DEFENSE, SECURITY AND STRATEGIES

U.S. MARITIME COUNTERPIRACY EFFORTS

DEFENSE, SECURITY AND STRATEGIES

Additional books in this series can be found on Nova's website under the Series tab.

Additional e-books in this series can be found on Nova's website under the e-book tab.

DEFENSE, SECURITY AND STRATEGIES

U.S. MARITIME COUNTERPIRACY EFFORTS

GILLES HORNES
EDITOR

nova publishers
New York

Library of Congress Cataloging-in-Publication Data

ISBN: 978-1-63463-334-5

Published by Nova Science Publishers, Inc. † New York

CONTENTS

PREFACE

The United States has long been a leader in maritime security, including in countering the threat of piracy. Since 2009, the United States has organized and led the international effort that has seen successful pirate attacks decline off the coast of Somalia dramatically. The Counter Piracy and Maritime Security Action Plan provides clear strategic guidance for counter-piracy efforts and outlines that the United States will use all appropriate instruments of national power to repress piracy and related maritime crimes. The Plan focuses on three core areas: Prevention of Attacks, Response to Acts of Maritime Crime, and Enhancing Maritime Security and Governance; and provides specific frameworks for the Horn of Africa and Gulf of Guinea regions. These frameworks establish the tailored and specific methodology for these regions and provide guidance on how the United States will respond to the regional threats associated with the varying geographic, political, and legal environments. This book discusses the U.S. maritime counterpiracy efforts.

Chapter 1 - Piracy and maritime crime continues to threaten ships off the Horn of Africa's east coast and in the Gulf of Guinea off Africa's west coast, putting seafarers in harm's way and costing governments and industry billions of dollars in ransom, insurance, and protective measures. The types and causes of piracy and maritime crime, as well as the African states' ability to address the problem in the two regions, differ. To help U.S. agencies coordinate efforts, the NSCS developed an interagency plan in 2008 to prevent, disrupt, and prosecute piracy off the Horn of Africa in collaboration with industry and international partners. GAO was asked to evaluate U.S. counterpiracy activities.

This report: (1) assesses how piracy off the Horn of Africa has changed since our 2010 review, and describes U.S. efforts to assess its counterpiracy actions, given any changing conditions; and (2) identifies trends in piracy and maritime crime in the Gulf of Guinea and U.S. efforts to address them, and evaluates the extent to which the United States has assessed its counterpiracy efforts in the Gulf of Guinea. GAO reviewed plans, activities, and data from 2007 through 2013 and interviewed officials from U.S. agencies, international partners, and industry, selected as a nongeneralizable sample for their involvement in counterpiracy activities.

Chapter 2 - The United States has long been a leader in maritime security, including in countering the threat of piracy. Since 2009, the United States has organized and led the international effort that has seen successful pirate attacks decline off the coast of Somalia dramatically.

The Counter Piracy and Maritime Security Action Plan provides clear strategic guidance for counter-piracy efforts and outlines that the United States will use all appropriate instruments of national power to repress piracy and related maritime crimes. The Plan focuses on three core areas: Prevention of Attacks, Response to Acts of Maritime Crime, and Enhancing Maritime Security and Governance; and provides specific frameworks for the Horn of Africa and Gulf of Guinea regions. These frameworks establish the tailored and specific methodology for these regions and provide guidance on how the United States will respond to the regional threats associated with the varying geographic, political, and legal environments.

Chapter 3 - Pirate attacks in the waters off Somalia and the Horn of Africa, including those on U.S.-flagged vessels, have brought renewed international attention to the long-standing problem of maritime piracy. According to the International Maritime Bureau (IMB), at least 219 attacks occurred in the region in 2010, with 49 successful hijackings. Somali pirates have attacked ships in the Gulf of Aden, along Somalia's eastern coastline, and outward into the Indian Ocean. Using increasingly sophisticated tactics, these pirates now operate as far east as the Maldives in good weather, and as far south as the Mozambique Channel. Hostage taking for ransom has been a hallmark of Somali piracy, and the IMB reports that more hostages, over 1,180, were taken at sea in 2010 than any year since records began; over 86% of those were taken by Somali pirates.

The increase in pirate attacks off the Horn of Africa is directly linked to continuing insecurity and the absence of the rule of law in war-torn Somalia. The absence of a functioning central government there provides freedom of action for pirates and remains the single greatest challenge to regional security. The lack of law enforcement capacity creates a haven where pirates hold hostages during ransom negotiations that can last for months. Some allege that the absence of Somali coastal security authorities has allowed illegal international fishing and maritime dumping to go unchecked, which in turn has undermined coastal communities' economic prospects, providing economic or political motivation to some pirates. The apparent motive of most pirate groups, however, is profit, and piracy has proven to be lucrative. Somalia's "pirate economy" has grown substantially in the past two years, with ransoms now averaging more than $5 million. These revenues may further exacerbate the ongoing conflict and undermine regional security.

The annual cost of piracy to the global economy ranges between $7 and $12 billion, by some estimates. The U.N. Security Council has issued a series of resolutions since 2008 to facilitate an international response, which is coordinated by a multilateral Contact Group. The Council has authorized international navies to counter piracy both in Somali territorial waters and ashore, with the consent of Somalia's Transitional Federal Government (TFG), and has also authorized, as an exemption to the U.N. arms embargo on Somalia, support for the TFG security forces.

Counter-piracy patrols by multinational naval forces near Somalia are intended to compliment mariners' self-protection measures. Increased patrols and proactive efforts by ships have reduced attacks in the Gulf of Aden, but the U.N. Secretary-General warns that "while the effectiveness of naval disruption operations has increased and more pirates have been arrested and prosecuted, this has not stopped piracy. The trend of the increased levels of violence employed by the pirates as well as their expanding reach is disconcerting." Some suggest that a perception of impunity exists among pirates and financiers; nine out of ten Somali pirates apprehended by naval patrols are reportedly released because no jurisdiction is prepared to prosecute them.

The United States has sought to prevent, disrupt, and prosecute Somali piracy through a range of interagency and multilateral coordination and enforcement mechanisms. The Obama Administration has initiated a new "dual track" policy toward Somalia, where some contend that international efforts to build a credible central authority have failed. Congress has examined options to address piracy both diplomatically and militarily. Congress appropriates funding and provides oversight for policy initiatives with implications for piracy in the region, including maritime security assistance to regional governments, support to peacekeeping operations in Somalia, and funding for U.S. Navy operations. Congress continues to debate options for addressing pirate safe havens and improving the prospects for prosecution of pirate suspects.

In: U.S. Maritime Counterpiracy Efforts
Editor: Gilles Hornes
ISBN: 978-1-63463-334-5

Chapter 1

MARITIME SECURITY: ONGOING U.S. COUNTERPIRACY EFFORTS WOULD BENEFIT FROM AGENCY ASSESSMENTS*

United States Government Accountability Office

WHY GAO DID THIS STUDY

Piracy and maritime crime continues to threaten ships off the Horn of Africa's east coast and in the Gulf of Guinea off Africa's west coast, putting seafarers in harm's way and costing governments and industry billions of dollars in ransom, insurance, and protective measures. The types and causes of piracy and maritime crime, as well as the African states' ability to address the problem in the two regions, differ. To help U.S. agencies coordinate efforts, the NSCS developed an interagency plan in 2008 to prevent, disrupt, and prosecute piracy off the Horn of Africa in collaboration with industry and international partners. GAO was asked to evaluate U.S. counterpiracy activities.

This report: (1) assesses how piracy off the Horn of Africa has changed since our 2010 review, and describes U.S. efforts to assess its counterpiracy actions, given any changing conditions; and (2) identifies trends in piracy and maritime crime in the Gulf of Guinea and U.S. efforts to address them, and

* This is an edited, reformatted and augmented version of the United States Government Accountability Office publication, GAO-14-422, dated June 2014.

evaluates the extent to which the United States has assessed its counterpiracy efforts in the Gulf of Guinea. GAO reviewed plans, activities, and data from 2007 through 2013 and interviewed officials from U.S. agencies, international partners, and industry, selected as a nongeneralizable sample for their involvement in counterpiracy activities.

What GAO Recommends

GAO recommends that the NSCS, with the Secretaries of Defense and State, collaborate with the involved agencies to assess their efforts and to determine whether additional actions are needed to guide efforts in the Gulf of Guinea. The NSCS did not concur or non-concur with GAO's recommendations but provided an update on its planning activities.

What GAO Found

Piracy incidents off the Horn of Africa's east coast near Somalia have declined sharply since 2010, but U.S. agencies have not assessed their counterpiracy efforts as GAO recommended in 2010. Since 2010, the International Maritime Bureau (IMB) reports piracy incidents declined from 219 to 15 in 2013. Similarly, from 2010 to 2013 hostages taken by pirates declined from 1,016 to 34. Also, a World Bank report stated that total ransoms declined by 2012. Officials participating in counterpiracy activities from the Departments of Defense and State, among others, as well as shipping industry officials and international partners, attribute the decline to a combination of prevention, disruption, and prosecution activities. However, officials cautioned that this progress is tenuous, and discontinuing these efforts could allow piracy to resurge. Despite changing conditions, U.S. agencies have not systematically assessed the costs and benefits of their counterpiracy efforts. Agency officials stated that their decisions and actions are guided by discussions rather than formal assessments. GAO has previously noted that assessments of risk and effectiveness in an interagency environment can strengthen strategies and resource usage. As such, GAO's prior recommendations remain valid and could help U.S. agencies identify the most cost effective mix of efforts and prioritize activities as they respond to changing conditions and fiscal pressures while avoiding a resurgence in piracy.

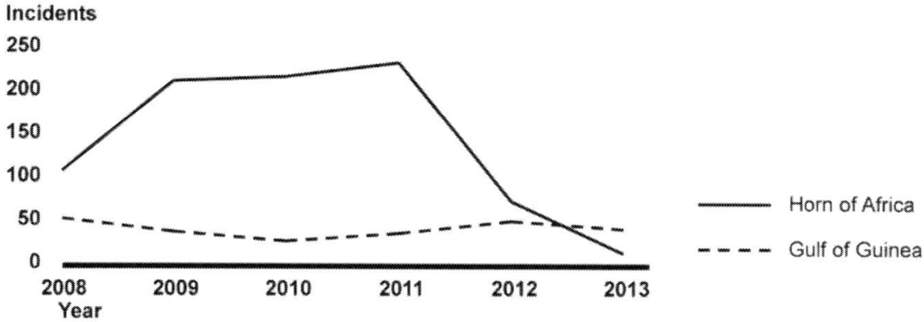

Source: GAO analysis of International Maritime Bureau data. | GAO-14-422

Reported Incidents of Piracy and Maritime Crime, 2008 through 2013.

Off the west coast of Africa, piracy and maritime crime has been a persistent problem in the Gulf of Guinea, as shown in the figure below. Although the United States has interagency and international efforts underway with African states to strengthen maritime security, it has not assessed its efforts or the need for a collective plan to address the evolving problem in the region. The U.S. role in addressing piracy in the Gulf of Guinea has focused on prevention, disruption, and prosecution, through training and assistance to African coastal states. However, according to U.S. agencies working in the region, the National Security Council Staff (NSCS) has not directed them to collectively assess their efforts to address piracy and maritime crime. An assessment of agencies' Gulf of Guinea efforts could strengthen their approach by informing the appropriate mix of activities to achieve the most effective use of limited resources, as well as help determine if additional actions are needed.

ABBREVIATIONS

AMLEP	African Maritime Law Enforcement Partnership
BMP	*Best Management Practices for Protection against Somalia Based Piracy*
CPCC	Counter-Piracy Coordination Center
CTF	Combined Task Force
DHS	Department of Homeland Security
DOD	Department of Defense
DOJ	Department of Justice
DOT	Department of Transportation

ECCAS	Economic Community of Central African States
ECOWAS	Economic Community of West African States
EU	European Union
FBI	Federal Bureau of Investigation
G8	Group of Eight
IMB	International Maritime Bureau
INL	Bureau of International Narcotics and Law Enforcement
IRTC	Internationally Recommended Transit Corridor
MOTR	Maritime Operational Threat Response
MSCHOA	Maritime Security Centre–Horn of Africa
NATO	North Atlantic Treaty Organization
NSC	National Security Council
NSCS	National Security Council Staff
ONI	U.S. Office of Naval intelligence
UN	United Nations
UNCLOS	United Nations Convention on the Law of the Sea

***

June 19, 2014

The Honorable John D. Rockefeller IV
Chairman
Committee on Commerce, Science, & Transportation
United States Senate

The Honorable Duncan Hunter
Chairman
The Honorable John Garamendi
Ranking Member
Subcommittee on Coast Guard and Maritime Transportation
Committee on Transportation and Infrastructure
House of Representatives

The Honorable Rick Larsen
House of Representatives

The Honorable Frank A. LoBiondo
House of Representatives

Piracy and maritime crime, including armed robbery, kidnapping, and hijackings, continues to threaten ships in the waters off the Horn of Africa and in the Gulf of Guinea, putting seafarers in harm's way and costing businesses and governments billions of dollars in ransoms, insurance, and protective measures. U.S. efforts to combat piracy and maritime crime involve multiple agencies from the Departments of Defense (DOD), Homeland Security (DHS), Justice (DOJ), State (State), Transportation (DOT), and the Treasury (Treasury) and are coordinated with international and industry partners. While maritime piracy is not a new threat, pirate attacks off the Horn of Africa started reaching unprecedented levels in 2008. At the same time, the persistence of attacks in West Africa's Gulf of Guinea—including the kidnapping of two Americans from a vessel in October 2013—have evolved with pirates venturing farther from shore and using more violent tactics.[1] According to DOD and State officials, piracy off the Horn of Africa stems from an ungoverned Somalia and has generally focused on hijacking ships transiting through open waters, while piracy in the Gulf of Guinea has generally focused on armed robbery of ships in territorial waters of sovereign states and has displayed less regard for the health and safety of its victims.

In September 2010, we issued a report examining U.S. efforts to address piracy off the Horn of Africa and found that the U.S. government had taken steps to implement the National Security Council's (NSC) *Countering Piracy off the Horn of Africa: Partnership and Action Plan* (Action Plan) by, for example, working with partners to conduct naval patrols, update ship security plans, and provide judicial capacity building to African states.[2] However, we found that many agencies could benefit from greater specificity in assigning roles and responsibilities, and from identifying the costs, benefits, and measures of effectiveness of their counterpiracy efforts, among other things.[3] We recommended that the NSC collaborate with the agencies to reassess and update its Action Plan; identify metrics; assess the costs, benefits, and effectiveness of U.S. counterpiracy activities; and clarify agency roles and responsibilities. In March 2011, we testified that piracy off the Horn of Africa continued to be a problem as pirates shifted tactics, and we reiterated our recommendations on actions the government could undertake to improve U.S. efforts.[4] As of June 2014, these recommendations have not been implemented and are discussed later in this report.

As piracy and maritime crime continues to evolve off both African coasts and the U.S. government faces fiscal pressures, you asked that we examine whether opportunities exist to leverage the cooperative efforts and strategies used to counter piracy off the Horn of Africa in addressing the problem of piracy and maritime crime in the Gulf of Guinea. Specifically, this report:

- assesses how piracy off the Horn of Africa in the East has changed since our 2010 report and describes U.S. efforts to assess counterpiracy actions, given any changing conditions; and
- identifies trends in piracy and maritime crime in West Africa's Gulf of Guinea and U.S. efforts to address them, and evaluates the extent to which the United States has assessed its counterpiracy efforts in the Gulf of Guinea.

To assess how piracy off the Horn of Africa has changed since 2010, we analyzed data from the International Maritime Bureau (IMB) and the U.S. Office of Naval intelligence (ONI) on reported piracy incidents, hostages taken, and ransom paid off the Horn of Africa from 2008 through 2013.[5] We discussed data collection methods, processes for data entry, and the steps taken to ensure reasonable accuracy of the data with both IMB and ONI. We determined the data to be sufficiently reliable for the purposes of this report. In addition, we met with DOD, DHS, DOJ, State, DOT, and Treasury officials; international partners; and representatives from insurance, shipping, and private security industry associations to discuss their involvement in counterpiracy activities such as developing best practices for protecting ships from pirate attack, working with the international Contact Group on Piracy off the Coast of Somalia, and participating in naval patrols off the Horn of Africa.[6] We met with officials from shipping industry associations that represent owners and operators from over 80 percent of the world's merchant fleet and describe themselves as providing a unified industry voice in the creation of industry policy and strategy; insurance industry associations whose members cover approximately 90 percent of the world's ocean-going tonnage; and a private security industry association that has over 180 members across 35 countries. While the statements of these industry officials cannot be generalized to the entire industries they represent, their perspectives provide valuable insight since each is actively involved in international collaborative efforts to combat piracy. To determine the extent to which the United States has assessed its counterpiracy actions as outlined in the 2008 Action Plan for countering piracy off the Horn of Africa, we reviewed the 2008 Action Plan, the 2005 *National Strategy for Maritime Security,* the 2007 *Policy for the*

Repression of Piracy and other Criminal Acts of Violence at Sea, relevant U.S. policies and laws, and United Nations (UN) Security Council resolutions. We also reviewed program documents such as briefings and meeting summaries and interviewed officials from DOD, DHS, DOJ, State, DOT, and the Treasury, as well as components including U.S. Naval Forces Central Command, the U.S. Coast Guard, and the Federal Bureau of Investigation (FBI), to discuss implementation of the Action Plan and the status of implementing recommendations from our September 2010 report to improve the plan.[7] We selected these departments and agencies because the Action Plan states they shall contribute to, coordinate, and undertake initiatives in accordance with the plan and they are members of the Counter-Piracy Steering Group established to oversee the implementation of the plan.

To identify trends in piracy and maritime crime in the Gulf of Guinea, we analyzed IMB and ONI data on piracy incidents—hijackings, boardings, attempts, ships fired upon, and kidnappings—reported from 2007 through 2013. As with the Horn of Africa data, we discussed the accuracy and reliability of the data with IMB and ONI officials and determined the data to be sufficiently reliable for the purposes of this report.[8] To evaluate U.S. efforts to address piracy and maritime crime in the Gulf of Guinea, we reviewed program briefings and meeting summaries and interviewed officials from the previously described U.S. agencies, international military partners, and partners from the insurance, shipping, and private security industries. The agencies, international partners, and industry associations we interviewed were those that we identified as contributors to ongoing counterpiracy activities in the Gulf of Guinea or those representing or insuring vessel owners and operators in the region. While the statements of the industry officials cannot be generalized to the entire industries they represent, their perspectives provide valuable insight since each is actively involved in international collaborative efforts to combat piracy. We compared agency efforts and their coordination against recommended practices in the *National Maritime Domain Awareness Plan* and the *Strategy to Combat Transnational Organized Crime* which are used to guide the efforts and, in general, call for risk-based assessments. A full description of our objectives, scope, and methodology can be found in appendix I.

We conducted this performance audit from June 2013 to June 2014 in accordance with generally accepted government auditing standards. Those standards require that we plan and perform the audit to obtain sufficient, appropriate evidence to provide a reasonable basis for our findings and conclusions based on our audit objectives. We believe that the evidence obtained provides a reasonable basis for our findings and conclusions based on our audit objectives.

BACKGROUND

Piracy Is a Recognized Global Issue

Under the 1958 Geneva Convention on the High Seas and the United Nations Convention on the Law of the Sea (UNCLOS), piracy consists of any of several acts, including any illegal act of violence or detention, or any act of depredation, committed for private ends by the crew or the passengers of a private ship and directed against another ship, aircraft, persons, or property onboard another ship on the high seas, or against a ship, aircraft, persons or property in a place outside the jurisdiction of any state.[9] According to both conventions, all states have the duty to cooperate to the fullest extent possible in the repression of piracy on the high seas or in any other place outside the jurisdiction of any state and are authorized to seize pirate ships or a ship under the control of pirates and arrest the persons and seize the property onboard on the high seas or in any other place outside the jurisdiction of any state.[10] When crimes that would constitute piracy are committed in the territorial waters of a coastal state, they are generally referred to as *maritime crime*. For the purposes of this report, we describe the criminal conduct in the Gulf of Guinea as *piracy and maritime crime* in order to include piracy on the high seas (i.e., outside the jurisdiction of any one sovereign state), as well as hijacking, armed robbery, kidnapping, and attempts at these crimes within the territorial waters of a state.

Piracy and maritime crime off the Horn of Africa and in the Gulf of Guinea affect countries around the globe. In 2013, over 42,000 vessels transited the waters off the Horn of Africa, which include some of the world's busiest shipping lanes. Within these waters, pirates target merchant vessels, fishing ships, and dhows.[11] Since 2008, the UN has adopted a number of United Nations Security Council resolutions related to countering piracy off the Horn of Africa.[12] Similarly, in 2011 and 2012, recognizing the Gulf of Guinea's critical shipping and global energy resources, the UN adopted resolutions that expressed deep concern about the threat that piracy and armed robbery at sea in the Gulf of Guinea pose to international navigation, security, and the economic development of states in the region.[13]

Piracy off the Horn of Africa Generally Differs from That in the Gulf of Guinea

The types of crime, vessel traffic, and coastal states' jurisdictional responses to address the piracy problem off the Horn of Africa and in the Gulf of Guinea generally differ, as does the U.S. response. DOD and State officials described the following as key differences:

- *Types of crime*: Piracy off the Horn of Africa is generally characterized by ransom-seeking, in which pirates attack ships for their crew, cargo, or the ship itself, which are often held hostage for months or years to obtain millions of dollars in ransom. In the Gulf of Guinea, piracy is generally characterized either as armed robbery—such as petroleum tanker hijackings to steal a ship's oil—or targeted kidnappings for ransom near or within the Niger Delta, according to DOD officials.
  Additionally, unlike the hostage-taking and high-dollar ransoms off the Horn of Africa that can result in months or years that a vessel and its crew are held, the kidnappings off the Niger Delta are for days or weeks, for thousands of dollars in ransom, and do not necessarily involve the hijacking of a vessel. In general, pirates hijack tankers and their crew only for the time it takes to offload the oil.[14]
- *Vessel traffic:* The nature of how vessels travel through the regions also differs. Sea traffic off the Horn of Africa is characterized by large, high-speed cargo vessels transiting through the Gulf of Aden and Indian Ocean. Piracy in this region generally involves pirates pursuing and boarding moving vessels. In contrast, in the Gulf of Guinea, commercial vessels generally are smaller and operate closer to shore, slowing down to make port calls and stopping at off-shore facilities in territorial waters or in the exclusive economic zones of coastal states. The slow speeds and stationary positions make these vessels vulnerable to piracy and maritime crime.
- *Jurisdiction and response:* U.S. efforts to combat piracy off the Horn of Africa and maritime crime in the Gulf of Guinea evolved in response to the particular characteristics of piracy and maritime crime in each region and the extent to which the United States has jurisdiction and coastal states have the capability to respond. For example, the UN authorized international militaries and organizations to enter Somali territorial waters and economic zones to conduct

counterpiracy operations and patrols as though they were international waters. The transitional and new Somali governments have relied on the assistance of international militaries since they are building maritime security capacities. Conversely, in the Gulf of Guinea, maritime security in territorial waters is under the authority of the respective recognized national governments in the region.[15]

Figures 1 and 2 show the number of attempted and successful pirate attacks off the Horn of Africa and in the Gulf of Guinea respectively from 2010 through 2013.

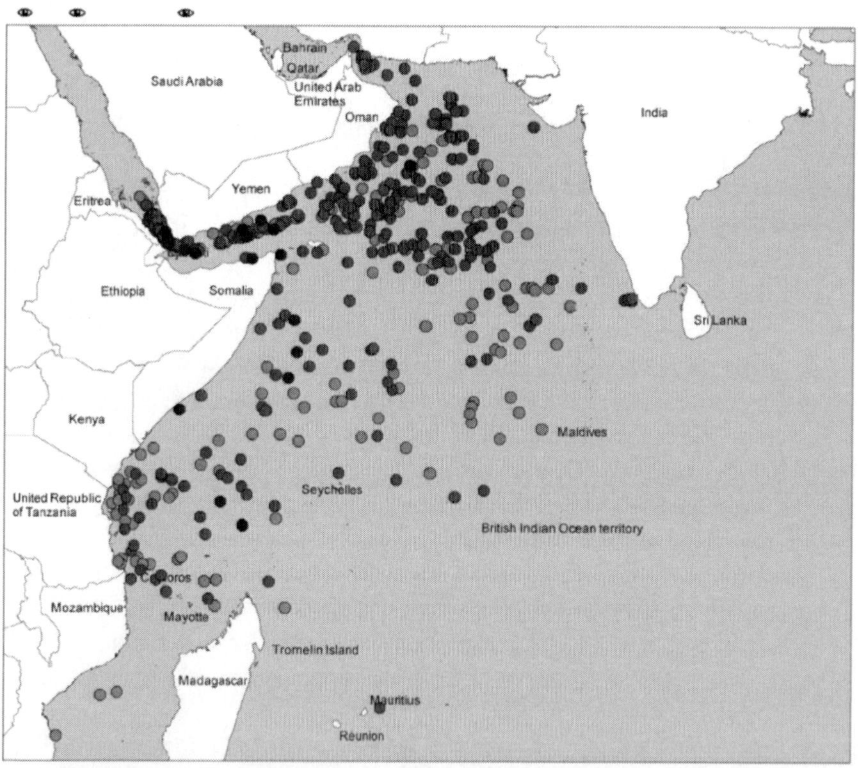

Source: GAO analysis of International Maritime Bureau data data): MapInfo (map). I GAO-14-422

See Appendix II for more information regarding Figure 1.

Figure 1. Attempted and Successful Piracy Incidents off the Horn of Africa, 2010 through 2013.

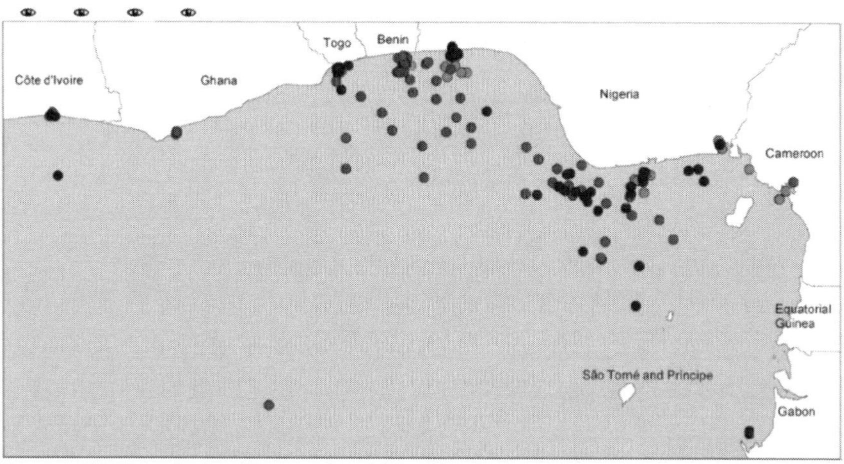

Source: GAO analysis of international Maritime Bureau data (data); MapInfo (map). | GAO-14-422.

Note: International Maritime Bureau (IMB) data are based on self-reporting by vessels and companies operating in the area made directly to IMB. According to Office of Naval Intelligence (ONI) data—which are aggregated from multiple data sources, (e.g. open source data such as media reports, IMB information, and all-source intelligence) and corroborated with other U.S. agencies and information—the actual number of incidents in the Gulf of Guinea is greater than what is reported to IMB. According to ONI and IMB officials, reasons for the variation between the two sets of data, include differences in categorization of incidents, validation of sources, underreporting, and differences in geographic scope. IMB data are presented in figure 2. A discussion of the data used in this report can be found in app I.

See Appendix II for more information regarding Figure 2.

Figure 2. Attempted and Successful Piracy and Maritime Crime Incidents in the Gulf of Guinea, 2010 through 2013.

In addition to the types of crimes, vessel traffic, and jurisdiction, other characteristics such as the reporting of incidents by vessel owners and operators and the ability of pirates to use land based safe havens for operations, among others, create differences between piracy off the Horn of Africa and piracy and maritime crime in the Gulf of Guinea. These differences are summarized in table 1.

Table 1. Piracy and Maritime Crime Characteristics in the Horn of Africa and Gulf of Guinea

Piracy characteristic	Horn of Africa	Gulf of Guinea
Location of incidents	International waters	Territorial and international waters
States with jurisdiction	All states have jurisdiction within Somali coastal waters and in international waters	Gulf of Guinea coastal states have jurisdiction within 0-12 nautical miles and all states have jurisdiction in international waters
Quality of incident reporting[a]	Good reporting of incidents	Underreporting of incidents
Nature of ship traffic	Transit the area at higher speeds and can avoid Somali coast	Make port calls to coastal states and are often slow moving or stationary
Pirate actors	Homogeneous actors (predominantly from five Somali clans)	Diverse set of actors (former militants, criminals, transnational criminal organizations)
Type of piracy business model	Hijacking vessels and crews	Mixed—hijacking, robbery, cargo theft, kidnapping for ransom
Violence to crews/hostages	Infrequent isolated incidents	Frequent incidents of violence throughout the event
Vessels targeted	Targets of opportunity, in particular ships that are "low and slow"	Intelligence-driven targets (i.e., pirates targeting vessels known to be carrying specific cargo such as oil) and some targets of opportunity
Pirate response to armed security teams	Pirates avoid engaging armed security teams	Pirates willing to engage armed security teams
Presence of safe havens	Safe havens off Somali coast serve as bases for operations	Limited safe havens to serve as bases for operations
Type of naval security forces in the region	International security forces provide naval patrols	Gulf of Guinea coastal states provide limited naval patrols

Source: GAO analysis of DOD, State, and UN information. | GAO-14-422

[a] According to DOD officials, the quality of incident reporting is their assessment based on the number of incidents they are aware of compared to the number that is reported.

The Response to Piracy off the Horn of Africa Involves Combined Efforts from U.S. and International Partners

Since 2008, the international community has taken steps to respond to piracy off the Horn of Africa, including patrols by the United States, NATO, the European Union (EU), and others in waters near Somalia; the establishment of international naval task forces with specific mandates to conduct counterpiracy operations; and the formation of a voluntary multilateral Contact Group to coordinate international counterpiracy efforts such as the development of industry practices and coordination of international law enforcement efforts. Recognizing that vibrant maritime commerce underpins global economic security and is a vital national security issue, the United States has also developed policies and plans to collaborate with its international partners and to mobilize a U.S. interagency response. In December 2008, the NSC published the Action Plan, which discusses countering piracy emanating from Somalia. The Action Plan directed the Secretary of State and Secretary of Defense to establish a high-level interagency task force—the Counter-Piracy Steering Group—to coordinate, implement, and monitor the actions contained in the plan. In addition, the NSC directed that DOD, DHS, DOJ, State, DOT, the Treasury, and the Office of the Director of National Intelligence undertake coordinated initiatives in accordance with the plan, subject to available resources.[16]

Various Efforts Have Reduced Piracy off the Horn of Africa since 2010, but the United States Has Not Updated its Action Plan

Piracy Incidents Off of the Horn of Africa Have Declined since 2010

Piracy activity off of the Horn of Africa has declined as indicated by the number of incidents reported, the number of hostages taken, and the amount of money paid in ransoms in 2013 as compared with recent years. In September 2010, we reported that successful and attempted piracy attacks off the Horn of Africa had risen from 30 in 2007 to 218 in 2009.[17] Our analysis of data provided by the IMB, which collects reported incidents from ship owners and operators, shows that the number of piracy incidents continued to rise to 235 in

2011, but declined thereafter to 15 total incidents in 2013, as shown in figure 3.[18]

At the same time, the number of hostages taken during pirate attacks rose from 815 in 2008 to 1,016 in 2010, but declined to 34 in 2013, as shown in figure 4.

As the number of hostages taken during piracy incidents rose, the amount of ransom money collected by pirates also increased. According to the UN Office on Drugs and Crime and the World Bank, low estimates of the total dollar amount of ransoms paid to free hostages rose from $2.4 million in 2007 to $151.1 million in 2011 but declined to $36.4 million in 2012.[19] While ransoms paid were an estimated average of $1.2 million in 2007, the estimated average amount rose to $4 million in 2012, as shown in figure 5. According to State Department officials, at of the end of 2013, there were at least 49 hostages from 11 countries held by Somali pirates.

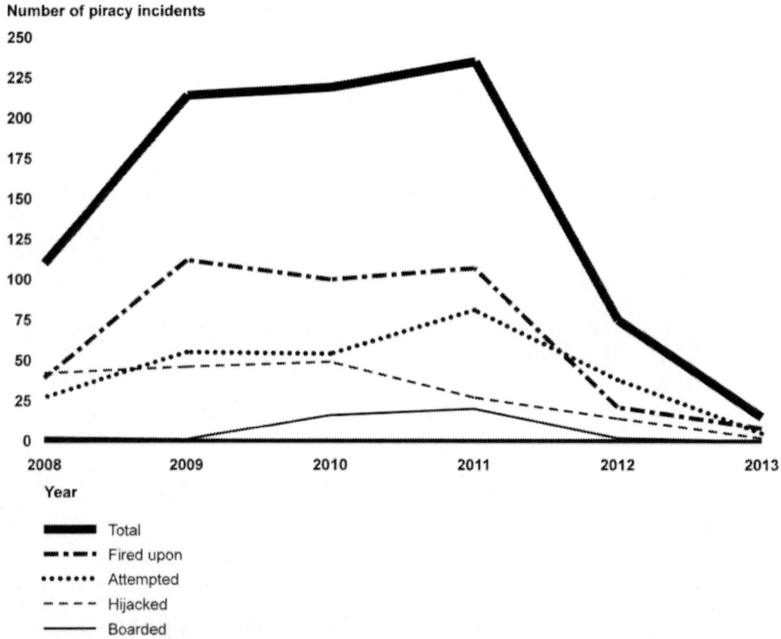

Source: GAO analysis of International Maritime Bureau data. | GAO-14-422

Figure 3. Piracy Incidents Reported off the Horn of Africa, 2008 through 2013.

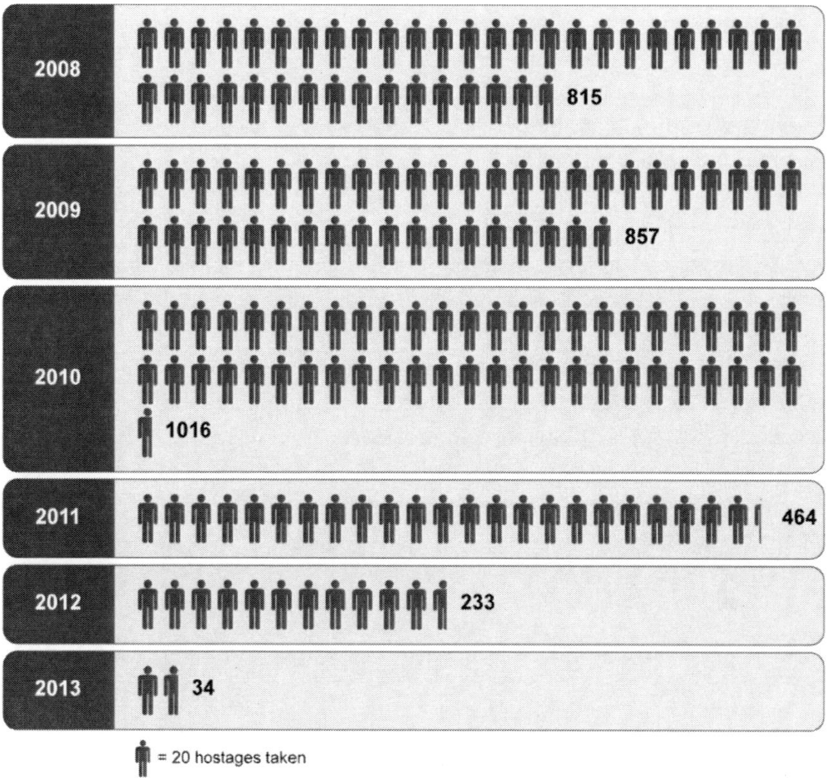

Source: GAO analysis of International Maritime Bureau data. | GAO-14-422

Note: Hostages taken include victims abducted from dhows, fishing ships, and merchant vessels. However, no hostages were taken from merchant vessels in 2013.

Figure 4. Hostages Taken In Horn of Africa Piracy Incidents, 2008 through 2013.

Officials Attribute the Decline in Horn of Africa Piracy to a Combination of Efforts to Prevent, Disrupt, and Prosecute

The Action Plan establishes the U.S. role in countering piracy as a collaborative one, seeking to involve all countries and shipping-industry partners with an interest in maritime security. DOD, DHS, DOJ, State, DOT, and the Treasury, in collaboration with their international and industry partners, have implemented steps in the Horn of Africa across the three lines of action established in the Action Plan, which are to: (1) prevent piracy attacks by reducing the vulnerability of the maritime domain, (2) disrupt acts of piracy in ways consistent with international law and the rights and responsibilities of coastal and flag states, and (3) ensure that those who commit acts of piracy are held accountable for their actions by facilitating the prosecution of suspected pirates.[20]

U.S. Efforts to Prevent Acts of Piracy

U.S. agencies, in collaboration with their international and industry partners have taken several steps to deter pirates and reduce the vulnerability of ships transiting off the Horn of Africa. DOD and State officials and representatives from each of eight shipping industry associations we met with emphasized that these prevention efforts work together and described the following as examples of key prevention efforts.

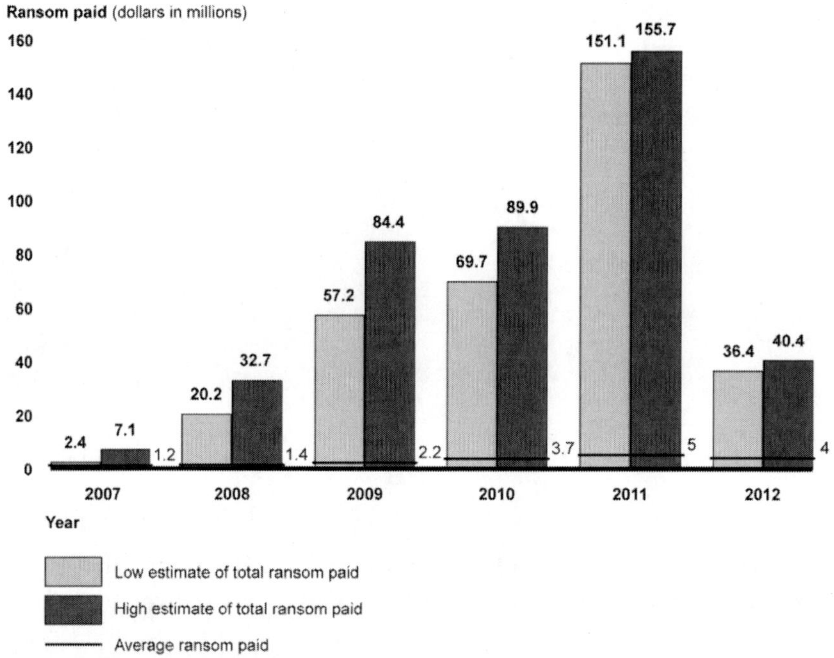

Source: World Bank 2013. | GAO-14-422

Figure 5. Estimated Total and Average Ransoms Paid in Piracy Incidents off the Horn of Africa, 2007 through 2012.

- *Working with Industry:* U.S. agencies have worked with industry partners to develop guidance and requirements for implementing counterpiracy efforts. For example, the Coast Guard issued Maritime Security (MARSEC) Directives that provide guidance to owners and operators of U.S. vessels on how to respond to emerging security threats.[21] These directives include practices that help to prevent pirate attacks and require that vessels operating in high risk waters update their vessel security plans to include security protocols for terrorism, piracy, and armed robbery against ships in high risk waters. Among other things, these plans cover the need for enhanced deterrence, surveillance and detection equipment; crew responses if a potential attack is detected or is underway; and coordination with counterpiracy organizations that could be of assistance. The practices are mandated for U.S. flag vessels operating in high risk waters and are also recommended for foreign flag vessels in the Coast Guard's Port Security Advisories and in the International Maritime Organization's (IMO) Maritime Safety Committee circulars.[22]

Additionally, the Coast Guard and DOT's Maritime Administration (MARAD) co-chaired Working Group 3 of the Contact Group on Piracy off the Coast of Somalia which focused on industry awareness. Through this working group, practices were developed and enhanced through the *Best Management Practices for Protection against Somalia Based Piracy* (BMP), developed by the working group's maritime industry representatives to deter, prevent, and deny incidents of piracy off the Horn of Africa. The BMP was introduced in 2008 as a joint industry strategy and has been updated based on lessons learned from investigated piracy incidents throughout the region. Version 4 of the BMP was issued in August 2011 and recommends 14 specific actions shipping companies can take to mitigate pirate activity while transiting high risk waters off the Horn of Africa. Examples of these ship protection measures include providing additional lookouts during watch periods, enhancing the ship's physical barrier, and establishing a safe point or secure citadel on the ship to ensure the safety of the crew and vessel during a pirate boarding. Use of the BMP is not mandatory; rather, officials from each of the eight shipping industry associations we interviewed describe the BMP as a tool kit of practices the ship's master can tailor to the situation and risks that the ship faces. Officials from an insurance industry association we met with stated that its members encourage and consider the implementation of the practices when pricing products based on steps that vessel owners have taken to mitigate risks.

Of the various implemented practices, officials from the six U.S. agencies engaged in counterpiracy activities and the eight shipping industry associations we interviewed describe the use of privately contracted armed security personnel on ships as a key factor in reducing the number of piracy incidents off the Horn of Africa. However, each of the eight shipping industry associations we interviewed stated that they do not want armed security teams to become a standard long term practice, primarily because of the hazards involved with the use of force and weapons aboard ships as well as the expense, with an average cost of about $5,000 per day for a four person security team. These officials added that, in comparison, requiring crew to continuously lookout for suspicious activity is a relatively low-cost measure when compared to deploying armed security personnel with a vessel – the burden of which could be too costly for smaller shipping companies. As security costs become a concern and the threat of piracy declines, DOD, EU, and NATO officials expressed concern that some in the shipping industry may seek to reduce the size and qualifications of the security teams as well as the hours they are deployed to protect the ship.

- *Strategic communication:* According to officials from DOD's AFRICOM, strategic communication from Somali radio stations is also an effective method of preventing piracy. These officials stated that the United States and its international partners have supported a partnership with Somali radio stations to bring awareness to the Somali public about the dangers of piracy and acts of abuse that hostages may endure.

U.S. Efforts to Disrupt Acts of Piracy

U.S. efforts to disrupt acts of piracy involve working with international partners to position resources to interdict pirates at sea and prevent the financing of pirates on land. The following were described by DOD, State, Treasury, EU, and NATO as examples of U.S. efforts that are intended to prevent acts of piracy.

- *Maritime coalition operations:* DOD, State, industry, EU, and NATO officials cited the presence of international navies in the region as a key factor in interdicting and disrupting pirate activity. Three multinational maritime coalition operations— the Combined Task Force (CTF) 151, EU Naval Forces (EU NAVFOR) Operation Atalanta, and NATO's Operation Ocean Shield[23]—along with independent deployments from countries outside of NATO and the EU such as China, India, Japan, and South Korea have worked to protect the waters off the Horn of Africa and the Internationally Recommended Transit Corridor (IRTC).[24] U.S. involvement in these activities is primarily through participation in CTF 151 and NATO's Operation Ocean Shield. DOD and State officials stated that these operations are effective in establishing a protective force in a region that is growing its own capabilities and has allowed the United States to build new partnerships with navies from around the world.

- *U.S. presence:* According to Navy officials, while as of 2013 the United States no longer regularly dedicates naval vessels to CTF 151, the U.S. presence plays an important role in fostering the participation of other countries in the task force. Additionally, the Navy may task ships from other missions, such as counternarcotics or counterterrorism, into the task force on a given day or for short periods to respond in an emergency if they are the closest or most appropriate—consistent with the overarching goal of preserving safety of life at sea. The Unites States has regularly provided, from 2010 through 2014, at least one ship in support of NATO's Operation Ocean Shield counterpiracy mission. As incidents of piracy have declined off the Horn of Africa, the number of steaming days has also declined, as shown in figure 6.
- *Disrupting pirate financing:* To help disrupt pirate revenue, the U.S. Treasury is authorized to block financial transactions of known pirate actors through the application of Executive Order 13536 when there is a nexus to U.S. interests.[25] Under this authority, Treasury may impose sanctions on individuals providing funds to known pirate actors and can block the transaction if it involves a U.S. financial institution. Officials from an insurance industry association we met with stated that ship owners can carry insurance policies that reimburse companies for ransom paid as a result of pirate attacks. According to Treasury officials, members of the U.S. and international shipping industry initially expressed concerns that the ransom paid and

reimbursed by their policies could be prohibited by the executive order. Treasury officials also stated that the order has specific application, is applied on a case-by-case basis, and, as of March 2014, had not been formally applied in response to a potential ransom payment.

U.S. Efforts to Facilitate Prosecutions of Suspected Pirates

The Action Plan aims to ensure that those who commit acts of piracy are held accountable for their actions by facilitating the prosecution of suspected pirates, and in appropriate cases prosecuting pirates in the United States. Officials from DOD, State, and DOJ described several examples of how the United States plays a role in making sure pirates are brought to justice.

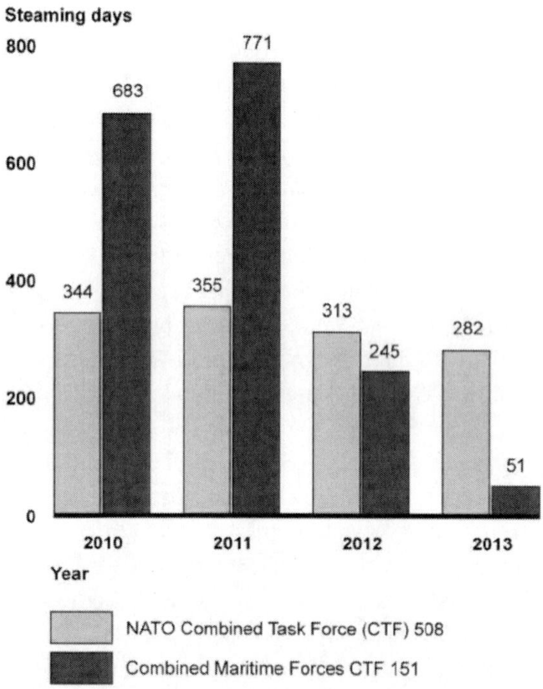

Source: GAO analysis of Department of Defense data. | GAO-14-422

Note: Steaming days are the days in which a naval vessel is actively patrolling the waters.

Figure 6. U.S. Naval Vessel Steaming Days in Horn of Africa Task Forces, 2010 through 2013.

- *Building law enforcement capabilities:* The United States helps expand law enforcement capabilities within the region through two key efforts. The Naval Criminal Investigative Service conducts investigations and has developed a manual that provides recommendations to law enforcement agencies investigating acts of piracy at sea. Last, the United States has contributed to a piracy database administered by INTERPOL that allows law enforcement agencies to access evidence connected to piracy incidents, although U.S. investigations are primarily focused on piracy incidents with a nexus to U.S. interests.[26]
- *Judicial capacity building:* U.S. agencies have also provided piracy-related judicial capacity-building assistance to countries in the region, such as Kenya and the Seychelles, for law enforcement and prosecutions. These activities have included establishing regional courts and building prisons in Somalia. Additionally, DOD, DOJ, and State have worked with international partners to ensure that pirates are tried and held accountable for their crimes by facilitating prosecution agreements. As of November 2013, among 22 nations, 1,130 Somali pirates had been detained for trial, were on trial, or had been convicted.
- *U.S. prosecutions*: The United States has jurisdiction to prosecute anyone who commits the crime of piracy as defined by the law of nations on the high seas and is later brought to or found in the United States.[27] U.S. government prosecutions have resulted in the conviction of at least 28 Somali pirates since 2010. In 2010, five men from Somalia were convicted of piracy and related offenses by a federal jury in what, according to DOJ officials, is believed to be the first piracy trial conviction in the United States since 1820 and is seen as the first in a series of government prosecutions aimed at slowing the spread of piracy off of Africa. In February 2013, a federal jury found five Somalis guilty of engaging in piracy and other offenses in connection with the attack on the Navy ship the USS Ashland. Additionally, in November 2013, a Somali pirate involved in the shooting of four Americans aboard a yacht off the coast of Somalia during a failed kidnapping attempt was sentenced to 21 life sentences for his role in their deaths.[28] Also, DOD, State, and DOJ officials stated that these prosecutions send a message that piracy carries serious consequences and may serve as a deterrent to others involved in piracy. However, DOJ and State officials told us that, especially in

cases where the hijacked vessel or crew has little or no connection to the United States, a more appropriate role for the United States would be to provide technical assistance to other countries in prosecuting pirates.

Appendix III provides a summary of the three lines of action and specific activities in the Action Plan. DOD, State, U.S. Coast Guard, DOJ, DOT, and the Treasury attribute the decline in piracy attacks to the collective implementation of these actions. Officials from these agencies noted that the efforts of governments and the industry practices work together to reduce vulnerabilities and prevent attacks. DOD, State, EU, and NATO naval officials as well as officials from the eight shipping industry associations we interviewed cautioned that discontinuing counterpiracy efforts could provide opportunities for piracy to resurge off the Horn of Africa. They stated that piracy off the Horn of Africa is a crime of opportunity driven by economic conditions in Somalia that have not been addressed. They noted that the practices in place have reduced the likelihood of a successful pirate attack by increasing the risk but the capability and motivation of pirates have not changed.

The U.S. Action Plan Has Not Been Updated as We Recommended in 2010

The Action Plan was published in December 2008 when piracy off the Horn of Africa was on the rise but has not been updated, as we recommended in 2010, to reflect changing dynamics in piracy, such as industry's use of armed security teams or the sharp decline in piracy incidents, or to implement recommendations we previously made to include elements of a strategic approach. The Action Plan was developed to identify and implement measures to suppress pirate activity off the Horn of Africa. Its intent was to respond to the growing threat and be mutually supportive of longer-term initiatives aimed at establishing governance, rule of law, security, and economic development in Somalia. In September 2010, we reviewed the Action Plan, which implements the *National Strategy for Maritime Security*[29] and the *Policy for the Repression of Piracy and other Criminal Acts of Violence at Sea*[30] as applied to piracy off the Horn of Africa. At that time, we found that the Action Plan had not been revised to reflect adapted piracy tactics and did not designate which agencies should lead or carry out most activities.[31] Additionally, we found that the

National Security Council Staff (NSCS) did not fully include characteristics of a strategic approach in the Action Plan, such as measures to evaluate the effectiveness of U.S. resources applied to counterpiracy, the identification of roles and responsibilities, or the cost of U.S. activities relative to the benefits they achieved.[32]

As a result, in September 2010 we recommended that the NSCS, in collaboration with the Secretaries of Defense, State, Homeland Security, Transportation, and the Treasury, as well as the Attorney General: (1) reassess and revise the Action Plan to better address evolving conditions off the Horn of Africa and their effect on priorities and plans; (2) identify measures of effectiveness to use in evaluating U.S. counterpiracy efforts; (3) direct the Counter-Piracy Steering Group to identify the costs of U.S. counterpiracy efforts including operational, support, and personnel costs; and assess the benefits, and effectiveness of U.S. counterpiracy activities; and (4) clarify agency roles and responsibilities and develop joint guidance, information-sharing mechanisms, and other means to operate across agency boundaries for implementing key efforts such as strategic communication, disrupting pirate revenue, and facilitating prosecution.[33] Since we issued our report in 2010, conditions have continued to change off the Horn of Africa in many ways since the Action Plan was developed in 2008. However, as of June 2014 the NSCS had not fully implemented the four recommendations from our September 2010 report as summarized in table 2.

- In commenting on a draft of this report, an NSCS official stated that the Action Plan is being updated through a global action plan, with a separate annex focusing on the Horn of Africa, but did not indicate whether the plan would include all of the elements in our recommendations. We continue to believe our recommendations have merit and should be implemented. While conditions affecting piracy have continued to evolve in the Horn of Africa since 2010, the 2008 Action Plan continues to guide U.S. efforts. Officials from each of the six agencies engaged in counterpiracy activities noted that current efforts are suppressing piracy off the Horn of Africa, but the results are tenuous and piracy could resurge without addressing its root causes. The Action Plan was developed at a time when U.S. policy focused on addressing problems in the absence of a functioning government in Somalia and without involving a U.S. presence in the country. With U.S. agencies and industry both having limited resources available for counterpiracy activities, we continue to believe that implementing our recommendations would be of value in understanding the costs and benefits and measuring the effectiveness of U.S. counterpiracy efforts. DOD, Coast Guard, DOJ, and State officials, as well as shipping industry officials, noted that the suppression of piracy has been based on a combination of government and industry counterpiracy activities, particularly the use of armed security teams on private vessels and the presence of naval patrols. However, U.S. agencies do not assess how industry practices and government resources could potentially offset each other's roles and associated costs.[34] As we concluded in September 2010, in an environment where government resource decisions directly affect costs incurred by the shipping industry and international partners, balancing risk reduction and benefits with costs should be emphasized.

Table 2. Update on Recommendation Implementation since September 2010

2010 Recommendation	Update since 2010
Reassess and revise the Action Plan to better address evolving conditions off the Horn of Africa and their effect on priorities and plans	Action Plan not updated. In September 2010, we recommended that the NSCS update the Action Plan because piracy was increasing and pirate tactics were changing. Since that time, conditions have continued to evolve off the Horn of Africa. Industry has made frequent use of embarked armed security teams. An internationally-recognized Somali federal government was established in August 2012 and responsibility for strategic communication was transferred to it. Piracy declined sharply in 2012 and 2013. EU NAVFOR and NATO counterpiracy operations off the Horn of Africa are set to expire by the end of 2016. State officials recognize that an updated Action Plan is needed and have provided input to the NSCS, but as of March 2014 they had not received guidance from the NSCS regarding any changes to counterpiracy plans or efforts. In commenting on a draft of this report, an NSCS official stated that a global action plan is being developed, with a separate annex focusing on the Horn of Africa and was expected to be issued in the summer of 2014.

2010 Recommendation	Update since 2010
Identify measures of effectiveness to use in evaluating U.S. counterpiracy efforts	Measures not established to assess counter piracy efforts. In September 2010, we recommended that the NSCS include measures of effectiveness in the Action Plan to provide direction for counterpiracy activities and information that could be used in strategic and resource-based decisions. During the course of this review, State officials told us the key measures are the number of hostages and ships hijacked, but they have not established formal measures and their decisions are generally guided by discussions rather than formal assessments. However, this information does not provide insight into which efforts are having the greatest effect in suppressing piracy.
Direct the Counter-Piracy Steering Group to identify the costs of U.S. counterpiracy efforts including operational, support, and personnel costs; and assess the benefits, and effectiveness of U.S. counterpiracy activities	U.S. counterpiracy costs and benefits not fully tracked. In September 2010, we reported that the United States is not collecting information to determine the most cost-effective mix of counterpiracy activities. During the course of this review, we obtained information from agencies identifying some costs related to their counterpiracy efforts. For example, the costs of counterpiracy efforts incurred by DOD peaked in 2011 at approximately $275 million but have declined to approximately $70 million in 2013.a State tracks funds used to operate its counterpiracy and maritime security functions, as well as foreign assistance provided to African countries. However, most agencies do not systematically track the costs of counterpiracy efforts or activities because these efforts and activities typically fall under a broader maritime security category. Further, the Counter-Piracy Steering Group has not identified the benefits of the various counterpiracy activities relative to their costs and resources.
Clarify agency roles and responsibilities and develop joint guidance, information-sharing mechanisms, and other means to operate across agency boundaries for implementing key	Agency roles and responsibilities defined for some tasks. In September 2010, we reported that agencies had made less progress in implementing action items in the Action Plan that involved multiple agencies than those that were the responsibility of one specific agency. Since that time, U.S. agencies have defined roles and responsibilities for applying the Maritime

Table 2. (Continued)

2010 Recommendation	Update since 2010
efforts such as strategic communication, disrupting pirate revenue, and facilitating prosecution	Operational Threat Response (MOTR) process to piracy incidents involving U.S. interests.b DOJ officials stated that the NSCS has also identified roles and responsibilities for transporting pirate suspects for prosecution. However, the NSCS has not established roles and responsibilities across all activities outlined in the Action Plan.

Source: GAO analysis of DOD, DHS, DOJ, State, Treasury, and NSCS information. | GAO-14-422.

[a] The costs include naval and air patrols, as well as contracted linguists.

[b] The MOTR is a separate presidentially approved Plan to achieve a coordinated U.S. Government response to threats against the United States and its interests in the maritime domain. The MOTR Plan contains operational coordination requirements to ensure quick and decisive action to counter maritime threats.

U.S. EFFORTSAIM TO ADDRESS PIRACY AND MARITIME SECURITY IN THE GULF OF GUINEA, BUT AN ASSESSMENT WOULD HELP INFORM EFFORTS AND DETERMINE THE NEED FOR ADDITIONAL ACTIONS

Piracy and Maritime crime in the Gulf of Guinea Is an Ongoing Problem, although Recent Incidents May Indicate Evolving Tactics and Capabilities

Piracy and maritime crime, primarily armed robbery at sea, oil theft, and kidnapping, is a persistent problem that continues to contribute to instability in the Gulf of Guinea. According to ONI data, incidents of piracy and maritime crime in the Gulf of Guinea rose from nearly 60 in 2010 to over 100 in 2011, and totaled more than 110 in 2013, as shown in figure 7. According to this data, incidents in 2013 included 11 vessel hijackings and 32 kidnappings. According to officials from AFRICOM, ONI, State, and the IMO, this recent rise in piracy and maritime crime in the Gulf of Guinea is part of a long-standing, persistent problem in the region. For example, according to DOD officials, the Gulf of Guinea was the most active region in the world for piracy in 2007, prior to the rise in pirate activity off the Horn of Africa. According to the IMB, the number of vessel-reported incidents in the Gulf of Guinea from 2007 through 2009 is similar to that of 2011 through 2013.[35] IMO officials added that, while the reported incidents indicate an ongoing, persistent problem, the number and frequency of incidents do not yet rise to the epidemic proportions that were seen off the Horn of Africa.

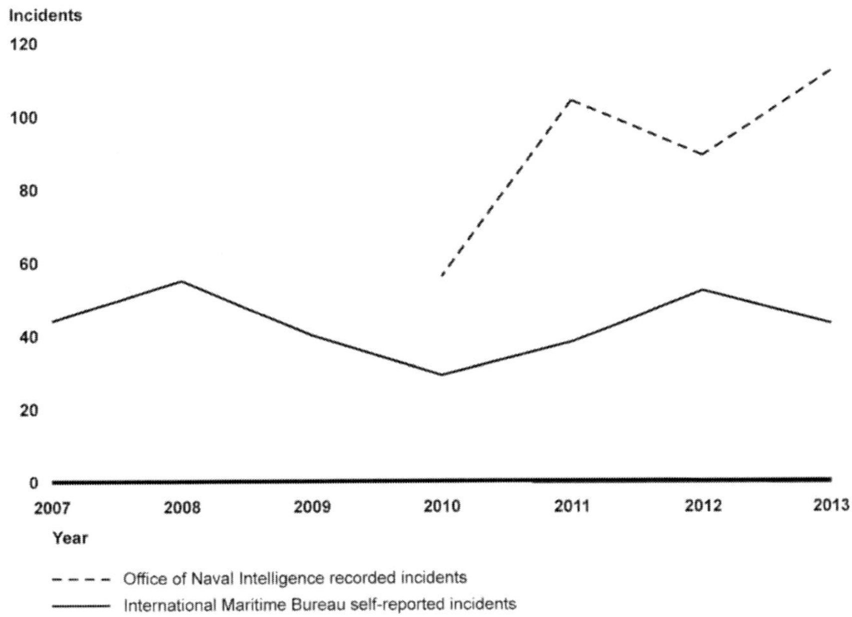

Source: GAO analysis of International Maritime Bureau and Office of Naval Intelligence data. | GAO-14-422

Notes: ONI data is aggregated from multiple data sources, (e.g., open source data such as media reports, IMB information, and all-source intelligence) and corroborated with other U.S. agencies and information. However, according to ONI officials, similar ONI data prior to 2010 is not available. IMB data is based on self-reporting by vessels and companies operating in the area made directly to IMB. According to DOD, State, industry, and IMB officials, there are several reasons for the variation between the two sets of data, including differences in categorization of incidents, validation of sources, under reporting, and differences in geographic scope. A discussion of the data used in this report can be found in appendix I.

Figure 7. Incidents of Piracy and Maritime Crime in the Gulf of Guinea, 2007 through 2013.

According to the U.S. Strategy to Combat Transnational Organized Crime and information from the U.S. Energy Information Administration, as well as the UN Security Council, piracy and maritime crime pose a threat to regional commerce and stability in the Gulf of Guinea. For example, according to the U.S. Energy Information Administration, while Nigeria has the second largest amount of proven crude oil reserves in Africa, as of December 2013, exploration activity there was at its lowest levels in a decade as a result of rising security problems related to oil theft, onshore pipeline sabotage, and piracy and maritime crime in the Gulf of Guinea, as well as other investment and government uncertainties.

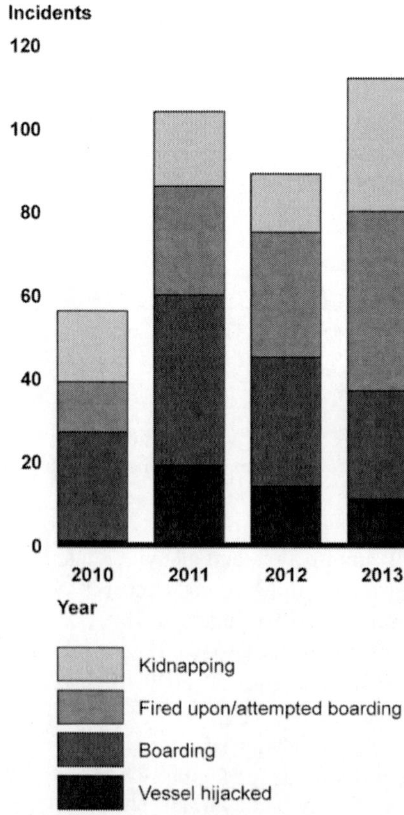

Source: GAO analysis of Office of Naval Intelligence data. | GAO-14-422

Figure 8. Types of Piracy and Maritime Crime Incidents in the Gulf of Guinea, 2010 through 2013.

Moreover, incident data since 2010 shows that piracy is moving farther off shore, prompting concerns that these trends may continue. According to officials from AFRICOM, ONI, and State, and according to IMB data as shown in figure 2 of this report, Gulf of Guinea piracy and maritime crime prior to 2011 have generally occurred in the coastal areas near Lagos or off the Niger Delta. However, recent attacks have taken place farther away from the waters off Nigeria, demonstrating a broader reach of pirates, as well as increasing the number of coastal states involved. For example, since 2011, several tanker hijackings were reported farther west than previously observed, off Togo and Cote d'Ivoire, according to ONI officials. Further, a July 2013 tanker hijacking off the coast of Gabon, and a similar incident off Angola in January 2014 represent, as of March 2014, the southernmost occurrences in which vessels were hijacked and sailed to Nigeria to offload the stolen oil cargo. According to AFRICOM officials, the ability to conduct such hijackings, which involve difficult maneuvering of large vessels across swaths of open water while conducting oil bunkering operations, illustrates that these maritime criminals may be increasingly capable of complex and long-range operations.[36]

The types of piracy and maritime crime in the Gulf of Guinea fluctuate from theft of petroleum products and other cargo to include a greater proportion of kidnappings for ransom. According to ONI and AFRICOM officials, while the total number of incidents has remained relatively constant since 2011, they have observed a recent increase in the proportion of kidnappings. Specifically, incidents of kidnapping increased from 14 incidents (or 16 percent of attacks) in 2012, to 32 incidents (or 29 percent of attacks in 2013), as shown in figure 8.[37] Further, combined with the higher levels of violence seen in the Gulf of Guinea as compared to the Horn of Africa, MARAD, State, and all eight of the shipping industry association officials we interviewed expressed that the increasing prevalence of kidnappings is a cause for concern.

The United States Has Ongoing Efforts to Strengthen Maritime Security in the Gulf of Guinea

According to AFRICOM officials, the objective of building partner capacity in the Gulf of Guinea, including strengthening maritime security, has long been part of U.S. military and diplomatic efforts in the region, even though the United States and international partners do not generally conduct naval patrols such as those conducted off the Horn of Africa.[38] For example, AFRICOM has conducted training and other efforts to strengthen regional security, including combating piracy and maritime crime, since its creation in 2008. According to AFRICOM, State, and U.S. Coast Guard Officials, while U.S. efforts in the Gulf of Guinea are informed by the region's specific geopolitical context, they also include efforts aimed to improve the prevention, disruption, and prosecution of piracy and maritime crime.

U.S. Efforts to Prevent Acts of Piracy and Maritime Crime

According to State and DOD officials, providing a permanent U.S. or international interdiction presence in the region is impractical because foreign nations do not have the authority to conduct military operations in another sovereign nation's territory and the need for limited naval resources to address other strategic priorities. However, as in the Horn of Africa, a variety of U.S. efforts are underway to help prevent acts of piracy and maritime crime in the Gulf of Guinea, including in the following areas:

- *Coordination of international activities and assistance:* According to DOD and State officials, facilitating collaboration and avoiding duplication is important to U.S. and international partners. To help achieve this, and in recognition of increasing concern in the region, an ad hoc Group of Eight (G8) group called the G8++ Friends of the Gulf of Guinea was established to conduct high-level coordination and discussion of international assistance efforts.[39] Further, State and AFRICOM officials said that as part of their planning process, AFRICOM holds planning conferences to solicit input from international partners, coordinate activities, and leverage resources. All U.S. officials we spoke with agreed that while the establishment of the Contact Group for the Horn of Africa was helpful in the absence of a functioning Somali government, in the case of the Gulf of Guinea, solutions must emerge from the region itself, and the role of the international community is to support and promote African-led initiatives. For example, the U.S., through DOD and State, has supported and facilitated the efforts of the two relevant African economic communities—the Economic Community of West African States (ECOWAS), and the Economic Community of Central African States (ECCAS)—to develop and lead efforts to prevent and suppress piracy. For example, according to AFRICOM and State officials,

AFRICOM and respective U.S. embassies supported the recent development of a code of conduct concerning the prevention of piracy, armed robbery, and other maritime crime, which was signed in June 2013 by leaders of the Gulf of Guinea coastal states.

- *Security advisories for U.S. vessels and ship protection measures:* MARAD provides security advisories to alert U.S. vessel operators transiting all over the world, and in August 2008, MARAD issued a maritime advisory warning of piracy and criminal activity against oil industry and other vessels by Niger Delta militants in Nigerian territorial waters. Additionally, in August 2010, MARAD warned that vessels operating near oil platforms in Nigerian waters were at high risk of armed attacks and hostage taking, and advised vessels to act in accordance with Coast Guard directives on security plans and risk assessments. Further, in March 2012, shipping industry organizations in coordination with NATO issued interim guidelines for protection against piracy in the Gulf of Guinea as a companion to their August 2011 BMP version 4 for the Horn of Africa region. Most recently, in July 2013, the U.S. Coast Guard directed U.S. vessels to revise their ship security plans and protective measures in response to continued attacks and lessons learned from investigations of recent incidents, including hijacking tankers for oil theft, acts of robbery, and kidnapping for ransom of vessel masters and officers from offshore oil exploration support vessels.

U.S. Efforts to Disrupt Acts of Piracy and Maritime Crime

Unlike off the coast of Somalia, where agreements authorize international forces, including the United States, to disrupt pirate attacks in territorial waters and dismantle pirate bases ashore, every Gulf of Guinea country possesses the sovereign rights to control its maritime and land borders. Accordingly, the U.S. role and the majority of its efforts pertain to training, security assistance, and coordination, including the following activities:

- *Bilateral equipment and training assistance to navies and coast guards:* According to IMO, DOD, and State officials, the development of regional countries' naval capabilities is critical to successfully fighting piracy and maritime crime in the Gulf of Guinea. Further, DOD officials told us that regional navies have either nascent or insufficient national maritime forces to independently combat the crime that occurs off their coasts, let alone that which may occur farther out to sea. To increase capabilities for regional maritime forces, State, in coordination with DOD, provides bilateral assistance and training to countries in the region. This includes approximately $8.5 million since 2010 in equipment and related training (e.g., vessels, engines, and maintenance training and parts) provided to countries in the greater Gulf of Guinea region to help build their maritime forces, according to State officials.[40] Additionally, according to State budget documents, since 2010, State has used its Africa Maritime Security Initiative to provide regional maritime security training and support through the DOD's Africa Partnership Station and requested $2 million for this effort in fiscal years 2013 and 2014.[41]

- *Training exercises to strengthen regional response capabilities:* In addition to equipment and training to build countries' maritime forces, AFRICOM and its naval component, U.S. Naval Forces – Africa provide multilateral training to improve regional maritime security operations capability, such as navy-to-navy exercises focused on maritime interdiction operations and response. For example, the annual Obangame Express exercise is a multi-country, multi-fleet exercise that implements various scenarios over several days. Begun as a proof of concept in 2010 with limited countries and vessels involved, the objectives of Obangame Express conducted in February 2013, according to AFRICOM, were focused on information sharing and interoperability among 10 Gulf of Guinea countries, the ECCAS Combined Maritime Center, ECOWAS, as well as the United States and 4 international partners. The exercises involve combating and responding to various scenarios including oil bunkering, trafficking illegal cargo, illegal fishing, and piracy, and AFRICOM officials stated that future exercises already have commitments of expanded international and regional participation.

U.S. Efforts to Support Prosecution of Suspected Pirates and Maritime Criminals

According to the Action Plan, facilitating the prosecution and detention of pirates off the Horn of Africa is a central element of U.S. efforts to combat piracy in the region. However, as previously noted, the majority of Gulf of

Guinea maritime crimes occur within the territorial waters of one or more country and as a result are under their legal jurisdiction. As such, the U.S. role in prosecuting suspected criminals, like its role in prevention and disruption of attacks, is one of support and capacity building, such as the following efforts:

- *Maritime law enforcement training and prosecution:* According to DOD, State, and U.S. Coast Guard officials, much of the training the United States provides to maritime law enforcement in the Gulf of Guinea is similar to that provided in the Horn of Africa, and is used to combat a variety of crimes, such as narcotics trafficking, arms smuggling, human trafficking, and illegal fishing, as well as piracy. For instance, in West Africa, AFRICOM and the Coast Guard provide training including visit, board, search, and seizure skills and mentorship through the African Maritime Law Enforcement Partnership (AMLEP) program, which aims to strengthen countries' abilities to enforce their maritime laws. AMLEP targets illicit trafficking in drugs, arms, and humans, as well as counterpiracy issues and illegal fishing, and the program has resulted in the successful seizure and prosecution of illegal fisherman by African law enforcement officers in African waters, according to AFRICOM officials.
- *Judicial capacity building:* State's Bureau of International Narcotics and Law Enforcement (INL) has conducted a series of regional maritime criminal justice seminars. Specifically, INL and the Africa Center for Strategic Studies have hosted a series of Trans-Atlantic Maritime Criminal Justice Workshops, which provide an opportunity for regional law enforcement agencies to learn about maritime crime and related gaps in their judicial systems. This series of conferences included a June 2013 session for ECOWAS countries in Ghana, with the other conferences held in February 2013 in Cape Verde and February 2014 in Benin. Additionally, according to State officials, in 2013 the agency began discussions with the G8++ Friends of Gulf of Guinea to develop possible future U.S. programs to strengthen regional countries' capacity to investigate and prosecute cases of armed robbery at sea and piracy.[42]

The United States Has Not Assessed Piracy and Maritime Crime in the Gulf of Guinea

According to DOD and State officials, U.S. efforts to combat piracy and maritime crime in the Gulf of Guinea are guided by the same over-arching U.S. policies and security goals as the efforts to combat piracy off of the Horn of Africa. These policies include the 2007 *Policy for the Repression of Piracy and other Criminal Acts of Violence at Sea*, the 2011 *Strategy to Combat Transnational Organized Crime*, the 2012 *Strategy toward Sub-Saharan Africa*, the 2012 *National Strategy for Maritime Security*, and the 2013 *National Maritime Domain Awareness Plan.* For example, the Strategy to Combat Transnational Organized Crime outlines East and West African maritime security as regional priorities, specifically noting incidents of Somali piracy and oil theft and kidnapping of oil workers in the Gulf of Guinea. DOD and State officials emphasized that U.S. efforts are then developed in consideration of the particular contexts of each region. In the case of Somalia, the surge and intensity of the rising piracy problem, the specific nature of the crime, and the absence of a functioning government presented a crisis that warranted collective international action, as well as a U.S. plan to guide its contribution to this response. Alternatively, State, DOD, and Coast Guard officials we spoke with explained that because the context of maritime crime in the Gulf of Guinea, and thereby the U.S. efforts there, encompass a broader set of geopolitical issues and maritime crimes, creating a piracy-focused plan similar to the Action Plan in the Horn of Africa may not be appropriate.

While there is not a whole-of-government plan to guide maritime security efforts in the Gulf of Guinea, DOD, State, Coast Guard, and others continue to expand and coordinate their maritime security activities there, which range from individual boarding team trainings to broad judicial sector reform. DOD and State officials told us that as the United States and international partners look to expand efforts in the Gulf of Guinea, coordinating activities to achieve the most effective mix and efficient use of resources is increasingly important. For example, officials from U.S. Naval Forces – Africa stated that occasional duplication of training activities can happen, particularly as international partners increase their attention to the region. However, according to officials from the U.S. government agencies working in the region, the NSCS has not directed them to conduct a collective assessment of efforts to combat piracy and maritime crime that weighs the U.S. security interests, goals, and resources in the region against the various types of agency and international activities underway. Moreover, while individual agencies have conducted analysis regarding the incidents of piracy and maritime crime such as armed robbery and kidnapping in the region, there has not been a coordinated interagency appraisal of how the variety of existing and planned activities address U.S. policy objectives in the context of such a broad set of maritime crimes, from illegal fishing and oil theft, to arms trafficking and kidnapping of U.S. citizens from offshore supply vessels.

The *National Maritime Domain Awareness Plan* cites the importance of understanding new and emerging maritime challenges in the maritime domain, the development of solutions to address those challenges, and continuous reassessment using risk management principles. Further, the *Strategy to Combat Transnational Organized Crime* outlines a specific set of U.S. priority actions to combat transnational criminal threats such as piracy and maritime crime, one of which is to increase research, data collection, and analysis to assess the scope and impact of such crime and the most effective means to combat it.

Individual agencies may include some assessment information into their planning and evaluation processes but this information is specific to agencies and programs rather than the overall U.S. effort. For example, according to AFRICOM officials, it uses available information to assess the operating environment, such as demographic surveys, to develop indicators to help measure program effectiveness, or it may conduct an assessment of a partner country's naval capabilities to inform program design. However, the chief of the AFRICOM assessments directorate said this assessment process is relatively new for the command, and there are no known interagency efforts to leverage this information into a broader assessment of U.S. maritime security or counterpiracy efforts. Additionally, according to State officials from the Political-Military Affairs Bureau, while individual programs such as State's foreign military financing or other security assistance activities may conduct evaluations of their programs, it is not part of a broader assessment of State's regional maritime security activities.

Program guidance for other multi-agency international collaborative efforts—such as providing counternarcotics assistance to countries to disrupt drug production and trafficking—has also shown that assessing agencies' progress in meeting established goals can provide better information for decision making. Guidance for these efforts demonstrates how incorporating elements of a strategic approach such as evaluating performance measures and setting performance targets can provide oversight and guide management decisions about the allotment of program resources.[43] If a multi-agency collaborative plan, such as the Action Plan, was developed for the efforts that address piracy and maritime crime in the Gulf of Guinea, including elements of a strategic approach could help determine the best use of resources to meet its objectives.[44]

An assessment that identifies the various U.S. and international efforts underway to strengthen maritime security, examines the relationship of these efforts with the nature and scope of the problem in the region, and considers the geopolitical environment and other regional factors could help strengthen ongoing efforts to combat maritime crime, as well as inform the appropriate mix of activities in order to use resources most effectively. Further, such an assessment could help determine whether additional actions, such as developing an action plan or other guidance, is needed to align U.S. interagency efforts to better achieve national security goals. In commenting on a draft of this report, an NSCS official stated that a global action plan is being developed, with a separate annex focusing on the Gulf of Guinea, but did not indicate the extent to which the plan was based on an assessment of ongoing activities or would include elements of a strategic approach.

CONCLUSION

Since our September 2010 report on piracy off the Horn of Africa, the U.S. Government—as part of an international partnership—has continued to take steps outlined in the Action Plan to counter piracy. In 2013, piracy steeply declined off the Horn of Africa, but the gains are tenuous and piracy could easily resurge if the international coalition becomes complacent. Whether piracy incidents are rising or declining, it is important for the Action Plan to be updated to account for current circumstances. In addition, our current work indicates that the U.S. Government has not implemented additional steps we recommended to identify measures of effectiveness, identify costs and benefits, and clarify agency roles and responsibilities. We are not making any new recommendations regarding the Action Plan for the Horn of Africa, but we continue to believe that our 2010 recommendations remain relevant to the changing conditions, and acting on these recommendations would assist the NSCS—and DOD and State as the co-chairs of the Counter-Piracy Steering Group—in better assessing, planning, and implementing actions to counter piracy as it continues to evolve, and would help ensure that recent progress is sustained.

Meanwhile, piracy and maritime crime in the Gulf of Guinea has escalated and in 2013 surpassed the Horn of Africa in terms of incidents. The variety of

U.S. efforts by multiple government agencies to combat piracy in the region highlights the importance of having coordinated activities that combine the most effective mix of resources. Without a collective assessment of the scope and nature of the problem of piracy and maritime crime, particularly in the Gulf of Guinea where no such collective assessment has occurred, the U.S. may not be coordinating its efforts in the most effective or cost efficient manner. An assessment of the various U.S. and international efforts, as well as of the geopolitical environment and other regional factors could help determine what additional actions are needed to align all of the efforts underway. Furthermore, an assessment of whether and to what extent such actions, such as developing an action plan that would include elements of a strategic approach, is needed can guide decision making to address the evolving threat, coordinate resources and efforts, and prioritize maritime security activities in the Gulf of Guinea.

RECOMMENDATIONS FOR EXECUTIVE ACTION

To help ensure that efforts to counter piracy and maritime crime are coordinated and prioritized to effectively address the evolving threat, we recommend that the Assistant to the President for National Security Affairs, in collaboration with the Secretaries of Defense and State, work through the Counter-Piracy Steering Group or otherwise collaborate with the Secretaries of Homeland Security, Transportation, and the Treasury, and the Attorney General to

- conduct an assessment of U.S. efforts to address piracy and maritime crime in the Gulf of Guinea to inform these efforts and
- determine whether additional actions to address counterpiracy and maritime security, such as developing an action plan that includes elements of a strategic approach, are needed to guide and coordinate activities.

AGENCY COMMENTS AND OUR EVALUATION

We provided a draft of this report to DOD, DHS, DOJ, State, DOT, Treasury, and the NSCS for review and comment. DHS, DOJ, DOT, and

Treasury, did not provide official comments on our draft report and DOD and State deferred to the NSCS for comments on the recommendations. In an email from the NSCS dated June 12, 2014, the NSCS did not concur or non-concur with our recommendations, but provided information related to its current counterpiracy efforts.

Specifically, the NSCS stated that it is coordinating with departments and agencies through the interagency process to develop a global action plan for countering piracy, with separate annexes focusing on the Horn of Africa and the Gulf of Guinea. The updated plan will provide guidance to the federal government focusing on three core areas including: prevention of attacks, response to acts of maritime crime, and enhancing maritime security and governance. The plan will be forthcoming in the summer of 2014 and the Executive Branch will continue to evaluate maritime crime around the world and develop or refine guidance to account for evolving conditions in specific regions.

We are encouraged by the steps being taken by the NSCS in providing the federal agencies responsible for counterpiracy activities with an updated plan, but it is not clear to what extent the plan will include previously recommended elements of a strategic approach. The description of the plan appears to provide a needed update to the Action Plan given the changes in conditions off of the Horn of Africa. The updated plan also appears to be responsive to part of our recommendation to consider additional actions such as developing a similar plan for the Gulf of Guinea. However, the description of the plan does not address the extent to which it will include elements such as an assessment of costs and benefits, measures of effectiveness to evaluate counterpiracy efforts, and defined roles and responsibilities for the agencies involved in carrying out counterpiracy activities. Further, the description does not address the extent to which the updated plan is based on an assessment of ongoing counterpiracy activities in the Gulf of Guinea. We will monitor the situation and review the updated plan once it is released and will continue to monitor the NSCS's progress in planning and providing guidance for counterpiracy activities as well as DOD and State's progress in implementing the plan as co-chairs of the Counter Piracy Steering Group.

DOD, DHS, and DOJ provided technical comments on a draft of this report which have been incorporated as appropriate.

Stephen L. Caldwell
Director, Homeland Security and Justice

Chris P. Currie
Acting Director, Defense Capabilities and Management

APPENDIX I. OBJECTIVES, SCOPE, AND METHODOLOGY

This report assesses how piracy off the Horn of Africa has changed since 2010 and describes U.S. efforts to assess its counterpiracy actions, given any changing conditions; and identifies trends in piracy and maritime crime in the Gulf of Guinea and U.S. efforts to address them and evaluates the extent to which the United States has assessed its counterpiracy efforts in the Gulf of Guinea.

To assess how piracy off the Horn of Africa has changed since 2010, we analyzed data from the International Chamber of Commerce's International Maritime Bureau (IMB) and the U.S. Office of Naval intelligence (ONI) on reported piracy incidents, hostages taken, and ransoms paid off the Horn of Africa from 2008 through 2013.[45] We discussed data-collection methods, processes for data entry, and the steps taken to ensure the reliability of the data with both IMB and ONI officials. We collected information from both IMB and ONI on their processes for quality control, data verification, and how potential errors are identified and corrected. We also discussed variation between IMB and ONI data with officials from ONI and other Department of Defense (DOD) organizations, the Department of State (State), and IMB, who attributed differences in categorization of incidents, validation of sources, and geographic scope to the variation.[46] Officials stated that while values between ONI and IMB data may differ, IMB is a generally accepted data source for tracking global piracy incidents and suitably reflects general historical trends.[47] We determined the data to be sufficiently reliable for the purposes of describing the context, trends, and scope of pirate attacks off the Horn of Africa in this report. In addition, we met with U.S. agency officials, international partners, and representatives from insurance, shipping, and private security industry associations to discuss their involvement in counterpiracy activities such as developing best practices for protecting ships from pirate attack, working with the international Contact Group on Piracy off the Coast of Somalia, and participating in naval patrols off the Horn of Africa.[48] We met with officials from shipping industry associations that represent owners and operators from over 80 percent of the world's merchant fleet and provide a unified industry voice in the creation of industry policy and strategy; insurance industry associations whose members cover approximately 90 percent of the world's ocean-going tonnage; and a private security industry association that has over 180 members across 35 countries. While the statements of these industry officials cannot be generalized to the entire industries they represent, their perspectives provide valuable insight since each is actively involved in international collaborative efforts to combat piracy. To determine the extent to which the U.S. has assessed its counterpiracy actions as outlined in the 2008 *Countering Piracy off the Horn of Africa: Partnership and Action Plan* (Action Plan), we reviewed the Action Plan, the 2005 *National Strategy for Maritime Security*, the 2007 *Policy for the Repression of Piracy and other Criminal Acts of Violence at Sea*, relevant U.S. policies and laws, and United Nations Security Council resolutions. We also reviewed program documents including briefings and meeting summaries and interviewed officials from DOD, State, and the Departments of Homeland Security (DHS), Justice (DOJ), Transportation (DOT), and the Treasury, including components such as U.S. Naval Forces – Central Command, the U.S. Coast Guard, and the Federal Bureau of Investigation (FBI), to discuss implementation of the Action Plan and the status of our 2010 recommendations to improve the plan.[49] We selected these departments and agencies because the Action Plan states they shall contribute to, coordinate, and undertake initiatives in accordance with the plan.

To identify trends in piracy and maritime crime in the Gulf of Guinea we analyzed IMB data on actual and attempted piracy incidents from 2007 through 2013, and ONI data from 2010 through 2013. As with the IMB and ONI data pertaining to the Horn of Africa, we collected information on the quality control, verification, and safeguards from error and discussed the reliability of the data with officials from IMB, ONI, and State officials involved in maritime security initiatives in the Gulf of Guinea and determined the data to be sufficiently reliable for the purposes of this report. Because ONI data on the Gulf of Guinea is unavailable prior to 2010 we chose to present the IMB data from 2007 through 2013 alongside the ONI data to show trends over a broader period. In addition to data, we reviewed publicly available reports and documents regarding maritime security and piracy in the Gulf of Guinea from the United Nations Office on Drugs and Crime, the EU, and other multilateral and nongovernmental organizations. To evaluate U.S. efforts to address piracy and maritime crime in the Gulf of Guinea, as well as the extent to which the U.S. has assessed the need for a strategic approach for the region, we reviewed relevant U.S. and international policies and laws, such as the 2005 *National Strategy for Maritime Security*, 2007 *Policy for the Repression of Piracy and other Criminal Acts of Violence at Sea*, the 2008 Action Plan, the 2012 *Strategy toward Sub-Saharan Africa*, and United Nations Security Council resolutions pertaining to the Gulf of Guinea. We also compared agency efforts with U.S. policy priorities and requirements for conducting assessments outlined in the 2011 *Strategy to Combat Transnational Organized Crime* and the 2013 *National Maritime Domain Awareness Plan*, documents that guide U.S. maritime security efforts, including in the Gulf of Guinea.

For both of our objectives, we interviewed officials and, where appropriate, obtained documentation related to their activities off the Horn of Africa or in the Gulf of Guinea such as fact sheets, briefings, and meeting summaries from the following U.S. government agencies and offices, international entities, and U.S. and international industry and nongovernmental organizations:

Department of Defense

- Office of the General Counsel; Office of the Undersecretary of Defense for Policy, Office of the Deputy Assistant Secretary of Defense for Counter-Narcotics and Global Threats; and the Joint Staff J5 Strategic Plans and Policy Directorate
- Department of the Navy, as well as the Naval Criminal Investigative Service, and the Office of Naval Intelligence
- U.S. Africa Command (Germany) and its components U.S. Naval Forces – Africa and Combined Joint Task Force – Horn of Africa
- U.S. Central Command and its component U.S. Naval Forces – Central Command (Bahrain)

Department of State

- Office of the Legal Adviser for: Economic and Business Affairs; and Law Enforcement and Intelligence
- Bureau of African Affairs
- Bureau of Counterterrorism
- Bureau of Economic and Business Affair
- Bureau of European and Eurasian Affairs
- Bureau of International Narcotics and Law Enforcement Affairs
-

- Bureau of International Organization Affairs
- Bureau of Political-Military Affairs

Department of Homeland Security

- U.S. Coast Guard offices, including the National Defense Strategy Division, Maritime Security (Counterterrorism) Division, Office of International Affairs and Foreign Policy; Office of Commercial Vessel Compliance; Office of Budget and Programs; and the Intelligence Coordination Center
- U.S. Coast Guard representatives at other agencies, including U.S. Africa Command (Germany) and Patrol Forces Southwest Asia (Bahrain)

Department of Justice

- National Security Division; the Criminal Division's Narcotic and Dangerous Drug Section, International Criminal Investigative Training Assistance Program, and the Office of Overseas Prosecutorial Development Assistance Training
- Federal Bureau of Investigation

Department of Transportation

- Office of the General Counsel
- Maritime Administration: Office of the Associate Administrator for Environment and Compliance and its Office of Security; Office of the Chief Counsel; Office of International Activities

Department of the Treasury

- Office of General Counsel; Office of Terrorism and Financial Intelligence and its offices of Terrorist Financing and Financial Crimes and Foreign Assets Control; Financial Crimes Enforcement Network

International Government and Multilateral Organizations Include

- International Maritime Organization (United Kingdom) European Union Naval Forces (United Kingdom)
- Combined Maritime Forces (Bahrain)
- Shared Awareness and Deconfliction Meeting (observed in Bahrain)
- North Atlantic Treaty Organization (NATO) and the NATO Shipping Centre (United Kingdom)
- United Kingdom Foreign & Commonwealth Office (United Kingdom)

Industry Partners and Nongovernmental Organizations Include

- Baltic and International Maritime Council (BIMCO) Center for Strategic and International Studies
- Chamber of Shipping of America
- International Association of Dry Cargo Shipowners (INTERCARGO) International Association of Independent Tanker Owners (INTERTANKO)
- International Chamber of Shipping International Group of P&I Clubs
- International Maritime Bureau
- International Transport Workers' Federation (ITF) Japanese Shipowners' Association
- Lloyd's Market Association Maersk Line, Limited
- Oceans Beyond Piracy
- Oil Companies International Marine Forum (OCIMF)
- Royal Institute of International Affairs (Chatham House) Security Association for the Maritime Industry (SAMI)
- Society of International Gas Tanker and Terminal Operators Limited (SIGTTO)

We conducted this performance audit from June 2013 to June 2014 in accordance with generally accepted government auditing standards. Those standards require that we plan and perform the audit to obtain sufficient, appropriate evidence to provide a reasonable basis for our findings and conclusions based on our audit objectives. We believe that the evidence obtained provides a reasonable basis for our findings and conclusions based on our audit objectives.

APPENDIX II. ATTEMPTED AND SUCCESSFUL PIRATE ATTACKS OFF THE HORN OF AFRICA AND IN THE GULF OF GUINEA, 2010 THROUGH 2013

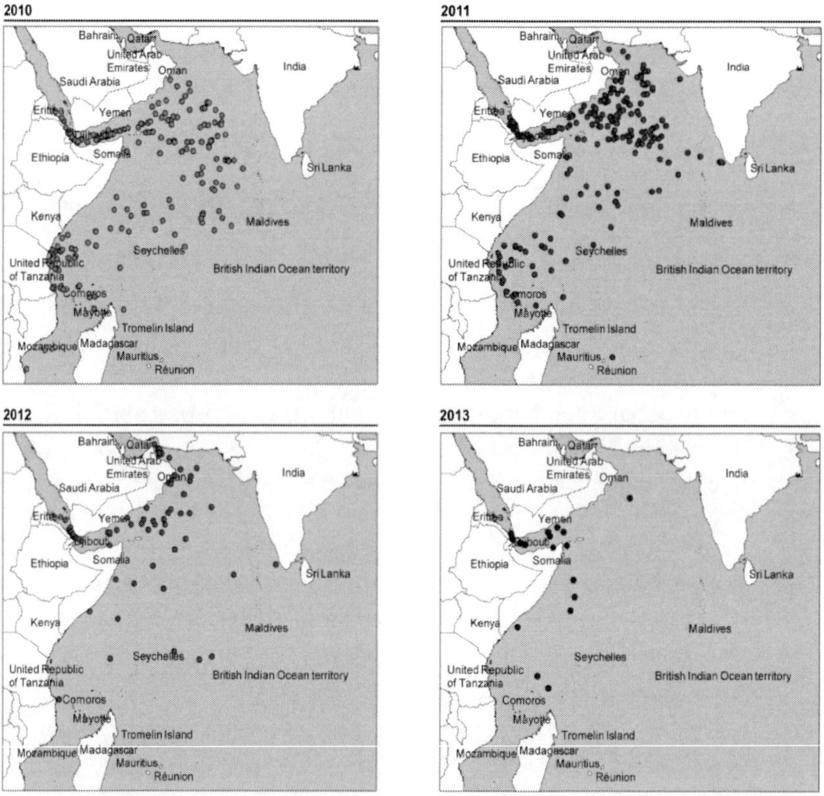

Source: GAO analysis of International Maritime Bureau data (data); MapInfo (map).| GAO-14-422

Figure 9. Attempted and Successful Pirate Attacks off the Horn of Africa, 2010 through 2013.

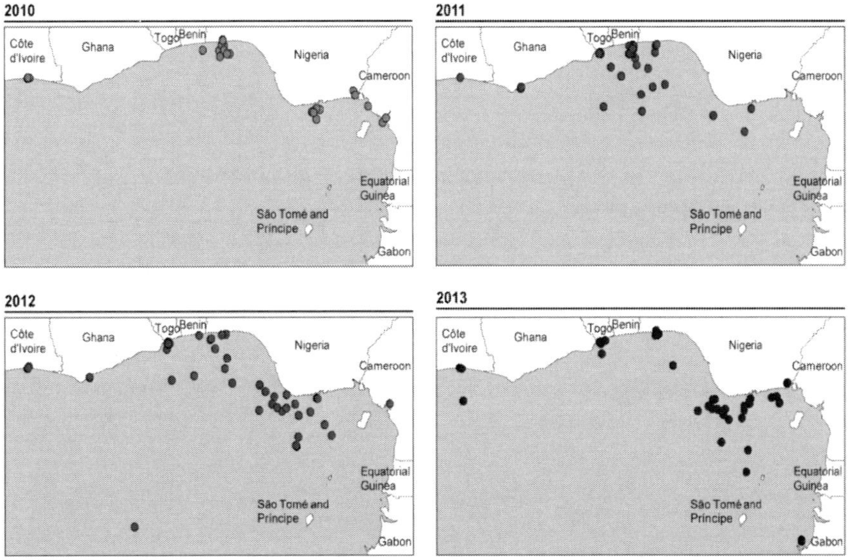

Source: GAO analysis of International Maritime Bureau data (data); MapInfo (map).| GAO-14-422.

Figure 10. Attempted and Successful Pirate Attacks in the Gulf of Guinea, 2010 through 2013.

APPENDIX III. INTERAGENCY PROGRESS IN IMPLEMENTING THE LINES OF ACTION IN THE NATIONAL SECURITY COUNCIL'S 2008 *COUNTERING PIRACY OFF THE HORN OF AFRICA: PARTNERSHIP AND ACTION PLAN*

In September 2010, we assessed the counterpiracy efforts of the United States government against the lines of action identified in the *Countering Piracy off the Horn of Africa: Partnership and Action Plan* (Action Plan).[50] These lines of action continue to guide the United States' efforts off the Horn of Africa. Table 3 summarizes our assessments from our September 2010 report and also provides updated information for each action since that time.[51]

Table 3. Interagency Progress in Implementing the Lines of Action in the National Security Council's (NSC) 2008 Action Plan

Tasks within each Line of Action	Status as of March 2014
Line of Action 1: Prevent pirate attacks by reducing the vulnerability of the maritime domain to piracy	
Establish and maintain a Contact Group	We assessed that the United States had made substantial progress on this action in 2010 by helping establish the Contact Group on Piracy off the Coast of Somalia, pursuant to UN Security Council Resolution 1851. Chaired by the United States in 2013, the voluntary group of over 80 countries, organizations, and industry groups facilitate the discussion and coordination of actions among states and organizations to suppress piracy off the coast of Somalia. The 2014 chair is the European Union.
Strengthen and encourage the use of the Maritime Security Patrol Area	We assessed that the United States had made substantial progress in this area in 2010 by working with international and industry partners. Since that time, the U.S. has continued to strengthen patrols by providing surface and air support. The U.S. has also actively encouraged practices such as registering with the regional coordination center and traveling in convoys. However, the United States has limited influence with ships that are not U.S. flagged.
Updating ships' security plans	We assessed that the Coast Guard had made substantial progress in this area in 2010 by approving piracy annexes to ship security plans for 100 percent of U.S.-flagged vessels identified as transiting high-risk waters, including those in the Horn of Africa. The Coast Guard has also issued Maritime Security (MARSEC) Directives that provide direction to owners and operators of U.S. vessels on how to respond to emerging security threats. The industry updated the Best Management Practices by releasing BMP4 in August 2011 to include recommended risk assessments and planning practices.
Strategic communication	The U.S. government made some progress on this in 2010 by issuing counterpiracy statements and supporting international efforts. Since 2010,

Tasks within each Line of Action	Status as of March 2014
	the United States began periodic anti-piracy radio programming in Somalia in coordination with local organizations, NATO, and the United Nations (UN). In November 2013, the Somali Government took over the responsibility for strategic communication.
Line of Action 2: Disrupt acts of piracy consistent with international law and the rights and responsibilities of coastal and flag states	
Support a regionally based Counter-Piracy Coordination Center (CPCC)	We assessed that this action was not applicable in 2010 because there were already reporting and monitoring functions being performed by other organizations. While the United States has not directly established a regional counterpiracy coordination center, the United States provides assistance to other centers. For example, the United Kingdom has established the Regional Fusion and Law Enforcement Center for Safety and Security at Sea in partnership with the Seychelles. State and DOJ have worked with the center to improve information sharing and coordination with INTERPOL. EU NAVFOR has also established the Maritime Security Centre – Horn of Africa (MSCHOA) to provide 24-hour manned monitoring of vessels transiting through the Gulf of Aden. While the United States supports the mission of these centers, State officials stated that it would be duplicative to establish one of its own and have no plans to do so.
Seize and destroy pirate vessels and related equipment and deliver suspected pirates to prosecuting states	We assessed that the U.S. government had made some progress in this area in 2010. Since that time, the United States and international forces have delivered over 1,000 piracy suspects for prosecution. The United States and international forces have also continued to seize vessels and equipment used for piracy.
Provide interdiction-capable presence	The U.S. Navy and Coast Guard had made substantial progress on this in 2010 and continue to contribute assets (such as ship and air patrols), leadership, and other support to coalition forces patrolling off the Horn of Africa. As piracy has decreased the United States has contributed fewer Naval patrols, but

Table 3. (Continued)

Tasks within each Line of Action	Status as of March 2014
	air patrols and other contributions have been more consistent.
Support shiprider[a] programs and other agreements	The U.S. government had made some progress on this in 2010 and continues to support other bilateral and regional arrangements to bolster regional capabilities to counter piracy. These include collecting and analyzing incident information, as well as facilitating assistance and a coordinated and effective information flow among partners. DOJ officials stated that U.S. agencies have not established shiprider programs and have no plans to do so because the U.N. has designated Somalia's territorial waters as international waters for the purpose of fighting piracy. Therefore they question the benefits of shiprider programs to facilitating prosecutions in this context.
Disrupt and dismantle pirate bases ashore	While the U.S. government had taken little or no action on this in 2010, the EU has since taken military action against pirate bases on the Somali coast. As a result, pirate bases have been largely dismantled or moved inland where DOD officials reported that they are a less effective threat.
Disrupt pirate revenue	The U.S. government had made some progress on this in 2010 as the President signed an executive order blocking assets of certain designated individuals, including two pirate financiers.[b] However, U.S. efforts to track financial assets or transactions are hampered because there are not financial institutions in Somalia.
Line of Action 3: Facilitate the prosecution of suspected pirates by flag, victim, and coastal states, and, in appropriate cases, the United States to ensure that those who commit acts of piracy are held accountable for their actions	
Conclude prosecution agreements	In 2010, we noted that the U.S. government had made some progress in this area. Since that time a prosecution agreement with Kenya has become less effective because Kenya's judicial system has become saturated with piracy suspects, according to State and Justice officials. The

Tasks within each Line of Action	Status as of March 2014
	United States has a prosecution agreement with the Seychelles.
Support the exercise of jurisdiction under the Convention for the Suppression of Unlawful Acts against the Safety of Maritime Navigation	In 2010, we noted that the U.S. government had made some progress in this area. The United States continues to exercise jurisdiction under the Convention for the Suppression of Unlawful Acts against the Safety of Maritime Navigation to prosecute pirates in the United States.
Support the use of other applicable international conventions and laws	Having made some progress in 2010, the United States has continued to exercise jurisdiction and prosecute, pursuant to 18 U.S.C. § 1651, 11 suspected pirates for attacks on the USS Nicholas and USS Ashland, as well as 15 suspected pirates tied to the hijacking of the S/V Quest which resulted in the murder of four Americans.
Enhance regional states' capacity to prosecute	While having made some progress on this in 2010, U.S. agencies continue to provide assistance to countries in the region for law enforcement and judicial capacity building and reform, which can include assistance related to maritime law enforcement and piracy. For example, the State Department has provided some foreign assistance funding to countries such as Kenya and the Seychelles, to help improve their judicial infrastructures. The United States also supports investigations and prosecutions, such as conducting Naval Criminal Investigative Service investigations aboard pirated vessels, and having U.S. Navy personnel provide testimony in foreign trials.

Source: GAO summary of the NSC *Countering Piracy off the Horn of Africa: Partnership and Action Plan.* | GAO-14-422.

[a] Shiprider programs involve embarking law enforcement officials from one country onto a ship of another country. The law enforcement official (shiprider) would be able to authorize the ship to pursue and apprehend a criminal suspect in the territorial waters of that official's country.

[b] Executive Order 13536, issued April 12, 2010, blocks all property and property interests within U.S. jurisdiction of persons listed in the Annex to the order and provides the authority for the Secretary of the Treasury, in consultation with the Secretary of State, to designate additional persons that threaten the peace, security, or stability of Somalia, which includes those who support or engage in acts of piracy off the coast of Somalia. See 75 Fed. Reg. 19,869 (Apr. 15, 2014). Property

and property interests within U.S. jurisdiction include property in the possession or control of any United States person in the United States or overseas. United States person is defined as "any United States citizen, permanent resident alien, entity organized under the laws of the United States or any jurisdiction within the United States (including foreign branches), or any person in the United States."

Appendix IV. Department of Defense Counterpiracy Costs, 2010 through 2013

During the course of our review, the Department of Defense provided information on the costs of its counterpiracy efforts as shown in table 4.

Table 4. Department of Defense Counterpiracy Costs Incurred from Calendar Years 2010-2013 (dollars in millions)

Counterpiracy effort	2010	2011	2012	2013
CTF 151 Surface	$161.1	$184.9	$53.5	$10.9
CTF 151 Air	17.9	23.9	33.5	16.0
CTF 508 Surface	61.7	63.2	52.7	40.0
Other[a]	2.5	2.5	2.5	2.5
Total	**$243.2**	**$274.5**	**$142.2**	**$69.4**

Source: GAO analysis of Department of Defense data. | GAO-14-422.

[a] The "other" category reflects the costs of contract linguists used in counterpiracy operations. Dollar values are fully-burdened costs incurred in a specific year.

End Notes

[1] According to State officials, on October 23, 2013, the Captain and Chief Engineer on the C-Retriever, an American owned oil-supply vessel, were kidnapped in the Gulf of Guinea and released sometime in the 3 weeks following the event.

[2] National Security Council, *Countering Piracy off the Horn of Africa: Partnership and Action Plan:* (Washington D.C. 2008).

[3] GAO, *Maritime Security: Actions Needed to Assess and Update Plan and Enhance Collaboration among Partners Involved in Countering Piracy off the Horn of Africa,* GAO-10-856 (Washington, D.C.: Sept. 24, 2010).

[4] GAO, *Maritime Security: Updating U.S. Counterpiracy Action Plan Gains Urgency as Piracy Escalates off the Horn of Africa* GAO-11-449T (Washington, D.C.: Mar. 15, 2011).

[5] IMB is a division of the International Chamber of Commerce established as a non-profit organization in 1981 to fight against all types of maritime crime and malpractice. IMB uses industry knowledge, experience, and access to contacts around the world to identify and investigate fraud, spot new criminal methods and trends, and highlight other threats to trade.

ONI is the division of the U.S. Navy that provides U.S. military, intelligence, and policy stakeholders with maritime intelligence including the analysis, production and dissemination of scientific, technical, geopolitical and military intelligence information.

[6] Pursuant to UN Security Council Resolution 1851 (2008), which encouraged states and regional organizations fighting piracy and armed robbery at sea off the coast of Somalia to establish an international cooperation mechanism to act as a common point of contact, the Contact Group on Piracy off the Coast of Somalia was established on January 14, 2009, to facilitate the discussion and coordination of actions among states and organizations to suppress piracy off the coast of Somalia.

[7] GAO-10-856.

[8] IMB data is based on self-reporting directly to IMB by vessels and companies operating in the area. According to ONI data—which is aggregated from multiple data sources, (e.g., open source data such as media reports, IMB information, and all-source intelligence) and corroborated with other U.S. agencies and information—the actual number of incidents in the Gulf of Guinea is greater than what is reported to IMB. According to ONI and IMB officials, reasons for the variation between the two sets of data, include differences in categorization of incidents, validation of sources, under reporting, and differences in geographic scope.

[9] In general, the degree to which a coastal state may exercise sovereignty and jurisdiction over its adjacent waters differs depending on its distance from the coast. Within a state's territorial sea (also referred to as its territorial waters), which extends not more than 12 nautical miles from its coast, is the area for which a state exercises sovereignty and jurisdiction. Within a state's contiguous zone—the area outside the territorial sea extending not further than 24 miles from a state's coast—the state may exercise control necessary to prevent infringement of laws and regulations within its territory or territorial sea. Further, within a state's exclusive economic zone—the area beyond and adjacent to the territorial sea, not extending beyond 200 nautical miles from the coastal baseline—the state has sovereign rights for the purpose of (and authority to exercise jurisdiction related to) exploring and exploiting, conserving and managing any natural resources, but through which all states generally enjoy the freedoms of navigation and overflight, among others. The "high seas" include all parts of the sea beyond national jurisdiction (i.e., beyond any states' exclusive economic zones). In this report, the term piracy refers to relevant acts committed in international waters—that is, anything beyond states' territorial seas—and maritime crime refers to such acts committed in a state's territorial sea.

[10] The conventions further provide that the courts of the state that carry out such seizures may decide upon the penalties to be imposed and may determine the action to be taken with regard to the ships, aircraft or property, subject to the rights of third parties acting in good faith.

[11] North Atlantic Treaty Organization (NATO) documents describe the term "dhow" as referring to a number of traditionally-constructed vessels used as the primary maritime commercial mode of transportation throughout the Red Sea, the Gulf of Aden, the Arabian Gulf, and the Indian Ocean. The structure and shape of dhows differentiate them from other types of merchant vessels and crew sizes vary between 5 and 30 individuals who, according to NATO's description, often do not have formalized seamanship or fishery training.

[12] For example, Resolution 1816, adopted in June 2008, authorized states to enter the territorial waters of Somalia for the purpose of repressing acts of piracy and armed robbery at sea. Resolution 2125, adopted in November 2013, renews the authorities and concerns raised in Resolution 1816 and other resolutions concerning piracy and armed robbery at sea with the backing of the Federal Government of Somalia that was formed in August 2012 following the end of the interim mandate of the Transitional Federal Government. Pursuant to Resolution 2125, international militaries and organizations may continue to operate in Somali territorial waters because the new government does not have the capability to protect its coastline.

[13] In October 2011 and in February 2012 the UN adopted Resolutions 2018 and 2039, respectively, urging Gulf of Guinea states to coordinate regionally and nationally, with help from international partners, to, among other things, develop and implement national maritime security strategies, including a legal framework for the prevention, and repression of piracy and armed robbery at sea, as well as for the prosecution of persons engaging in those crimes.

[14] According to DOD officials, as of September 2013, there is no linkage between the Gulf of Guinea piracy and violent extremist groups such as Boko Haram and oil and tanker theft is generally carried out by criminal organizations for financial gain.

[15] In June 2013, the governments of Angola, Benin, Burkina Faso, Burundi, Cameroon, Cape Verde, Central African Republic, Chad, Congo, Democratic Republic of Congo, Cote d'Ivoire, Gabon, The Gambia, Ghana, Guinea, Guinea Bissau, Equatorial Guinea, Liberia, Mali, Niger, Nigeria, Sao Tome and Principe, Senegal, Sierra Leone, and Togo signed the *Code of Conduct Concerning the Repression of Piracy, Armed Robbery Against Ships, and Illicit Maritime* Activities In West and Central Africa which calls for a regional framework to counter piracy and armed robbery at sea, including information-sharing and operational coordination mechanisms, among other things.

[16] A list of U.S. agencies, international partners, and industry partners involved in the response to piracy off the Horn of Africa as of September 2010 can be found in GAO-10-856 p.11 and 15.

[17] GAO-10-856.

[18] Reported incidents of piracy can vary based on the type of activity recorded and may include: (1) ships boarded, (2) ships hijacked, (3) attempted boardings of ships and (4) ships fired upon.

[19] World Bank. 2013. *Pirate Trails: Tracking the Illicit Financial Flows from Pirate Activities off the Horn of Africa.* A World Bank Study. Washington, DC: World Bank. doi:10.1596/978-0-8213-9963-7.

[20] The flag state is the country in which the vessel is registered. In general, flag states have the authority to enforce their own as well as international regulations, such as those relating to security standards, with respect to such vessels.

[21] Port Security Advisory (2-09) (Rev. 3) Maritime Security (MARSEC) Directive 104-6 (series), *Guidelines for U.S. Vessels Operating in High Risk Waters*. January 07, 2011.

[22] As a specialized agency of the UN, IMO is the global standard-setting authority for the safety, security and environmental performance of international shipping. Its main role is to create a regulatory framework for the shipping industry that is fair and effective, universally adopted and universally implemented. The Maritime Safety Committee is a technical body with representatives from each of the IMO member states which, among other things, considers and submits recommendations and guidelines on safety for possible adoption by the IMO Assembly.

[23] CTF 151 is a multinational naval task force, set up in 2009 with a specific mandate to respond to piracy attacks in the Gulf of Aden and off the eastern coast of Somalia. The EU NAVFOR maintains a counterpiracy presence in the region with its Operation Atalanta CTF 465. NATO maintains its counterpiracy presence in the region with its Operation Ocean Shield CTF 508.

[24] The IRTC is a defined geographic area in which ships are protected by transiting in groups at a common speed or in a planned convoy accompanied by a military vessel.

[25] See Exec. Order No. 13,536, *Blocking Property of Certain Persons Contributing to the Conflict in Somalia*, 75 Fed. Reg. 19,869 (Apr. 15, 2010).

[26] INTERPOL is an intergovernmental organization made up of 190 member countries that facilitates international police cooperation. Members work together to provide targeted training, expert investigative support, relevant data and secure communications channels, among other services.

[27] See 18 U.S.C. § 1651.

[28] In total, this prosecution resulted in the conviction of three pirates and guilty pleas from 11 others, all resulting in sentences of at least life imprisonment.

[29] The *National Strategy for Maritime Security* was created pursuant to National Security Presidential Directive NSPD-41 / Homeland Security Presidential Directive HSPD-13 (Dec. 21, 2004) and identified piracy as a threat the strategy intended to address.

[30] The *Policy for the Repression of Piracy and other Criminal Acts of Violence at Sea* states that it is the policy of the United States to repress piracy through, among other actions, "continu[ing] to lead and support international efforts to repress piracy and urge other states to take decisive action both individually and through international efforts."

[31] An assessment of progress made in implementing the *Action Plan* as of September 2010 can be found in GAO-10-856, p 19.

[32] We developed the characteristics of a strategic approach after our research examining legislative and executive mandates, including the Government Performance and Results Act of 1993; general literature on strategic planning and performance; and guidance from the Office of Management and Budget on the President's Management Agenda, found that there were no legislative or executive mandates identifying a uniform set of required or desirable characteristics for national strategies. Some of these characteristics include 1) a statement of purpose, scope, and methodology, 2) problem definition, 3) goals, priorities and performance measures, 4) costs and risk management, 5) roles, responsibilities, and coordination mechanisms, and 6) integration with other strategies. For a more detailed discussion, see *Combating Terrorism: Evaluation of Selected Characteristics in National Strategies Related to Terrorism*, GAO-04-408T (Washington, D.C: Feb. 3, 2004).

[33] Our recommendations were made to the National Security Staff which changed its name to the National Security Council Staff pursuant to Executive Order 13657, dated February 10, 2014.

[34] See appendix IV for a description of DOD counterpiracy costs, 2010 through 2013.

[35] As shown in figure 7, IMB reports a dip in incidents in the Gulf of Guinea in 2010. The United Nations Office on Drugs and Crime and the U.S. Energy Information Administration reported that a contributing factor to this decline was the 2009 amnesty and subsequent ceasefire between the Nigerian government and Niger Delta militants who had previously been responsible for attacks on the oil industry, to include kidnappings, acts of piracy, and attacks on pipelines and other oil facilities. However, according to the Energy Information Administration as well as State officials, delayed progress in implementing some of the conditions of the amnesty has in turn contributed to increased oil theft and other attacks in recent years.

[36] Oil bunkering is the process of offloading oil from one vessel onto another vessel.

[37] In the context of this report and data reported by ONI and IMB, kidnappings refer to those that have occurred, or were reported to have occurred. According to ONI and AFRICOM officials, such incidents would include scenarios in which oil industry personnel or others were kidnapped from offshore supply vessels or platforms and held for ransom, such as the case of the two U.S. oil industry personnel taken from the C-*Retriever* in October 2013 off the coast of Nigeria. However, according to AFRICOM and Naval Forces–Africa officials, kidnappings conducted against the oil industry, including those perpetrated by Nigerian militants over the last decade, also include onshore kidnappings, or kidnappings within the inland waters and river ways of the Niger Delta. Onshore or inland kidnappings are generally not included in this data, and ONI officials said they take steps to validate the data they report However, ONI officials told us that some self-reported or other data may unintentionally include such incidents.

[38] Maritime security activities in the Gulf of Guinea are primarily conducted by DOD and State, while others such as U.S. Coast Guard and MARAD also play a role.

[39] Since 1997, the G8 has been a forum for the governments of eight of the world's largest national economies—Canada, France, Germany, Italy, Japan, Russia, the United Kingdom, and the United States. In March 2014 it was announced that Russia would no longer take

part in the international group; however, it is unknown how this will effect G8-related organizations.

[40] According to State officials, this amount includes completed assistance programs with appropriated funding from fiscal years 2010 through2013; it does not include funding requests for fiscal year 2014 or activities with 2010 through 2013 funding that have not been fully executed. Additionally, State and AFRICOM officials said that their relevant Gulf of Guinea regional maritime security efforts, such as those provided through Africa Partnership Station, include West Africa countries not technically within the Gulf of Guinea.

[41] Africa Partnership Station, directed by AFRICOM and administered through U.S. Naval Forces – Africa, is the platform through which U.S. maritime security assistance— including that through State and Coast Guard—is provided to Africa. According to Naval Forces–Africa program documents, the fundamental purpose is to foster safety and security at sea to help promote prosperity and development ashore, and its broad areas of effort include combating trafficking in North and West Africa, securing energy infrastructure and maritime transportation in the Gulf of Guinea, and countering Somalia-based piracy. AFRICOM officials stated this effort has grown from an individual U.S. training effort to a coordinated, international set of activities. For example, according to Naval Forces–Africa, in 2013 all ship contributions for Africa Partnership Station activities were from partner nations.

[42] The United States also engages in a variety of judicial sector reform and bilateral governance programs intended to strengthen national judicial systems in Nigeria and other countries in the region, which includes but is not specifically aimed toward maritime law enforcement and prosecution capabilities, according to State officials.

[43] GAO, *Counternarcotics Assistance: U.S. Agencies Have Allotted Billions in Andean Countries, but DOD Should Improve Its Reporting of Results*, GAO-12-824 (Washington, D.C.: July 10, 2012).

[44] GAO-10-856. Elements of a strategic approach that could benefit such a plan include those previously recommended for the Action Plan to combat piracy off the Horn of Africa including defined agency roles and responsibilities; measurable goals and objectives linked to agency activities; a mechanism to assess the collective effectiveness, costs, and benefits of U.S. interagency activities; and a process to revise the plan as necessary to address evolving conditions, assessments of U.S. efforts, and priorities.

[45] The IMB collects its data on piracy incidents through its Piracy Reporting Centre. According to the IMB, the primary functions of the center are: to be a single point of contact for ship masters anywhere in the world who are under piratical or armed robbery attack; to immediately relay information received to local law enforcement agencies requesting assistance; and to immediately broadcast the information to all vessels in the region in order to increase overall domain awareness.

[46] We reviewed unclassified ONI data that is aggregated from multiple information sources (e.g., all-source data such as company- or vessel-provided information, media reports, and IMB data, as well as other U.S. and international partner entities such as MARAD, NATO, and the United Kingdom Maritime Trade Organization) and corroborated with other U.S. Government entities. IMB data is based on self-reporting of actual and attempted incidents by vessels and companies directly to IMB's Piracy Reporting Centre.

[47] IMB officials told us there is the potential for underreporting with their data because they rely on ship officials to provide the information, and the extent to which individuals are willing to report incidents can vary.

[48] Pursuant to UN Security Council Resolution 1851 (2008), which encouraged states and regional organizations fighting piracy and armed robbery at sea off the coast of Somalia to establish an international cooperation mechanism to act as a common point of contact, the Contact Group on Piracy off the Coast of Somalia was established on January 14, 2009, to facilitate the discussion and coordination of actions among states and organizations to suppress piracy off the coast of Somalia.

[49] GAO, *Maritime Security: Actions Needed to Assess and Update Plan and Enhance Collaboration among Partners Involved in Countering Piracy off the Horn of Africa,* GAO-10-856 (Washington, D.C.: Sept. 24, 2010).

[50] GAO, *Maritime Security: Actions Needed to Assess and Update Plan and Enhance Collaboration among Partners Involved in Countering Piracy off the Horn of Africa,* GAO-10-856 (Washington, D.C.: Sept. 24, 2010).

[51] In our September 2010 report, we assessed the efforts of U.S. agencies using three levels of progress: (1) substantial progress, (2) some progress, and (3) little or no progress.

In: U.S. Maritime Counterpiracy Efforts
Editor: Gilles Hornes
ISBN: 978-1-63463-334-5

Chapter 2

UNITED STATES COUNTER PIRACY AND MARITIME SECURITY ACTION PLAN*

Executive Office of the President

PURPOSE

Presidential Policy Directive 18 (PPD-18)[1] established United States Government policy on Maritime Security and provided for the development of scalable, flexible frameworks on specific maritime issues to guide and clarify roles and responsibilities for strategic goals of the United States. This document:

- Affirms the vital national interest in global maritime security and articulates United States Government policy for countering piracy, robbery at sea, and related maritime crime;
- Provides the overarching guidance to develop objectives to enhance maritime security in other regions of the world as required based on evolving and emerging threats; and
- Supersedes the Countering Piracy off the Horn of Africa: Partnership and Action Plan[2].

* This is an edited, reformatted and augmented version of a document issued by the White House, Office of the Press Secretary, June 2014.

Background and Overview

This Plan implements the National Strategy for Maritime Security[3] (Strategy) and the Policy for the Repression of Piracy and other Criminal Acts of Violence at Sea[4] (Policy). The Strategy affirms the vital national interest of the United States in maritime security and recognizes that nations have a common interest in achieving two complementary objectives: facilitating the vibrant maritime commerce that underpins economic security; and protecting against piracy, robbery at sea, and related maritime crime.

Our Policy provides that we shall "continue to lead and support international efforts to repress piracy . . . and urge other States to take decisive action both individually and through international efforts."[5] Through this Plan, the United States will seek to involve all nations, international organizations, industry, and other entities that have an interest in maritime security to take steps to repress piracy and related maritime crime. An integrated and comprehensive approach, through international coordination and cooperation, will advance objectives that enhance the global economy and promote freedom of the seas.

The nations of the world have long considered pirates to be universal enemies of mankind. Under customary international law, as reflected in the 1982 Law of the Sea Convention, every nation has jurisdiction to prosecute a suspected pirate for the crime of piracy, regardless of any connection between the State and the suspected pirate, the vessel, or the victims. Our interdependent and interconnected global society revolves around a world economy that depends upon maritime shipping. Governments must collaborate with international organizations and the shipping industry to confront and repress any persistent threat to global commerce.

Piracy and related maritime crime continue to plague mariners throughout the world and will continue to pose obstacles to the lawful use of the maritime domain. Due to changing conditions around the world, this Plan and its annexes will be periodically reviewed and updated to reflect United States Government policy regarding countering piracy and related maritime crime. As required, scalable, flexible annexes will be developed to address regional maritime criminal activities and coordinate U.S. and international policies to prevent, suppress, and prosecute these crimes effectively.

Flag, victim, and coastal States all have a stake in repressing piracy and related maritime crime. The United States will continue to foster international cooperation and integration among nations, international organizations, and industry, and to support and encourage affected States to exercise jurisdiction, including efforts to build justice-sector capacities. The United States will provide appropriate investigative and logistical support and assistance to other foreign States involved in response to acts of piracy and related maritime crime. When appropriate, the United States will prosecute persons or entities involved in piracy and related maritime crime.

Strategic Vision

The United States will use all appropriate instruments of national power to repress piracy and related maritime crime. The United States will seek to strengthen regional governance and rule of law to maintain the safety and security of mariners, preserve freedom of the seas, and promote the free flow of commerce through lawful economic activity.

Policy Priorities

The United States will continue to be a leader in combating piracy and related maritime crime. The United States, like most nations, relies heavily on international trade, secure global navigation, and unhindered legitimate commerce. Piracy and related maritime crime endanger ocean commerce and transportation, interfere with freedom of the seas, impede the lawful flow of commerce, and undermine regional stability.

Piracy and related maritime crime endanger maritime interests on a global scale, and countering this threat is a shared global responsibility. The United States will continue to collaborate with States and international and regional organizations, including the maritime industry and nongovernmental organizations, to develop greater resources and authorities to combat piracy and related maritime crime, and maximize the coordination of our efforts.

Combating piracy and related maritime crime requires the judicious use of all the tools of national power, including diplomatic, economic, social, military, intelligence, law enforcement, and judicial measures. A decisive and effective response to criminal activity and its perpetrators sends an important message of deterrence but requires coordination among all departments and agencies of the United States Government, as well with international partners. The primary efforts of the United States should focus on preventive actions, interruption of piracy acts, and building maritime security and governance capacity in affected States to hold pirates accountable.

It is the policy of the United States to repress piracy and related maritime crime, consistent with national law and international obligations, and to collaborate with other nations in this effort. The United States Government will:

- Reduce the vulnerability of the maritime domain to piracy and related maritime crime;
- Prevent pirate attacks and related maritime crime against U.S. vessels, persons, and interests, as well as those of our allies and partners;
- Interrupt and terminate acts of piracy and related maritime crime consistent with international law and the rights and responsibilities of coastal, flag, and other States;
- Ensure that those who commit acts of piracy and related maritime crime are held accountable for their actions by facilitating the prosecution of suspected pirates and ensure that persons committing maritime crime are similarly held accountable by regional, flag, victim, or littoral States or, in appropriate cases, the United States;
- Preserve the freedom of the seas, including all the rights, freedoms, and uses of the sea recognized in international law;
- Protect ocean commerce and transportation;
- Continue to lead and support international efforts to combat piracy and related maritime crime and urge other States to take decisive action both individually and through international efforts;
- Build the capacity and political will of regional States to combat piracy and related maritime crime, focusing in particular on creating institutional capacity for governance and the rule of law; and
- Strengthen national law to better enable successful prosecution of all members of piracy-related criminal enterprises, including those involved in financing, negotiating, or otherwise facilitating acts of piracy or related maritime crime.

Although overarching policy priorities remain the same, the ways and means to respond to threats will vary according to geographic, political, and legal environments. The annexed frameworks will establish the tailored and specific methodology for different regions, but will focus on three primary areas: Prevention of Attacks, Response to Acts of Maritime Crime, and Enhancing Maritime Security and Governance.

IMPLEMENTATION

The Maritime Security Interagency Policy Committee, or its successor, will lead the interagency process to accomplish the following tasks:

- Oversee the development and implementation of maritime frameworks for the preventive actions and response by the United States Government to piracy and related maritime crime that threaten the safety of the global maritime transportation system, framed on the following principles:
    - Prevention of Attacks – The first and best defense against piracy and related maritime crime, as shown through best management practices, is to reduce the vessel's risk and susceptibility to attack and to be prepared for a potential assault. Industry, ship owners, and mariners that operate in high-risk regions are best situated to prepare vessels before an attack occurs.
    - Response to Acts of Maritime Crime – Piracy and related maritime crime must not be ignored. A rapid and effective response will deter future criminal acts. These measures are designed to be implemented by affected mariners, security services, regional or affected nations, and/or international coalitions.
    - Enhance Maritime Security and Governance – A lack of shore-side governance and the failure of governments to deploy adequate maritime security measures is a primary factor that allows piracy and related maritime crime to flourish. These objectives are intended primarily for the United States and international partners to facilitate the development of regional governance by States and the adoption of rule of law by their citizens.
- Review existing U.S. laws against or relating to piracy and related maritime crime and, if necessary, prepare for consideration appropriate amendments to those U.S. laws to enhance our ability to prosecute individuals in U.S. courts who commit acts of piracy and related maritime crime, as well as those who aid and abet or otherwise facilitate such acts; and
- Build international cooperation, consistent with the International Outreach and Coordination Strategy of the National Strategy for

Maritime Security,[6] to enhance the ability of other States to combat piracy and related maritime crime and to support U.S. counterpiracy actions.

Annex A: Framework for Combating Piracy and Enhancing Maritime Security off the Horn of Africa

Annex B: Framework for Combating Piracy and Enhancing Maritime Security in the Gulf of Guinea

UNITED STATES COUNTER PIRACY AND MARITIME SECURITY ACTION PLAN – ANNEX A

Framework for Combating Piracy and Enhancing Maritime Security off the Horn of Africa

Background

In the early nineties, following the collapse of Somalia's government and economy, Somali-based pirates began attacking vessels and ransoming crews for private gain. Due to its location near the Gulf of Aden, a strategic maritime corridor, these actions greatly influenced maritime transportation routes and operations, costing the global economy about $18 billion dollars in increased trading costs. The lack of regional stability, coupled with corruption, further facilitated the spread of piracy off the Horn of Africa (HOA), as criminals had little disincentive or constraint to discontinue the lucrative practice. The increase in the pirates' wealth led to the expansion of their infrastructure and capacities on land.

Somali piracy involves hijacking vessels and kidnapping crew for ransom. Generally, cargo is not stolen and hostages are rarely killed. The fatalities that do occur are typically a result of severe mistreatment or neglect at the hands of the captors. Hijacked ships and crew are held as long as necessary to obtain financial payoffs, in many cases for years. A single pirate attack can affect the interests of numerous countries, including the flag State of the vessel, the nations represented by those seafarers taken hostage, regional coastal States, as well as the nation-States of the vessel owners, of the cargo destination, and of the transshipment locations.

Nearly 12 percent of the world's petroleum passes through the Gulf of Aden, one of the world's most important waterways. Pirate attacks undermine confidence in global sea lines of communication, weaken or undermine the legitimacy of affected States, threaten the legitimate revenue and resources essential to the rebuilding of Somalia, increase maritime insurance rates and cargo costs, increase the risk of environmental damage, and endanger the lives of seafarers who may be injured, killed, or taken hostage by pirates for ransom.

The international community, with strong leadership by the United States, has made great strides since 2008 in countering piracy off the HOA. Through the concerted efforts of the international Contact Group on Piracy off the Coast of Somalia (CGPCS), piracy off the HOA has dropped to its lowest levels since 2006. Yet, maritime piracy emanating from the under-governed shores of Somalia still threatens maritime trade in this strategically vital region of the world. The conditions that allowed piracy to flourish still exist in Somalia today. Most of the pirate criminal networks and their shore-based infrastructure likely remain intact. This annex implements the U.S. policy to foster international cooperation and integration among all nations, international organizations, industry, and other entities that have an interest in maritime security to ensure the full range of lawful and timely actions necessary to combat piracy and criminal activity off the HOA.

Overview of the Threat

Somali piracy involves hijacking vessels and kidnapping crew and passengers for ransom. Pirates attack targets of opportunity in the Red Sea, the Gulf of Aden, the Gulf of Oman, and the Indian Ocean. Typically, pirates armed with small arms and rocket-propelled grenades use outboard powered skiffs to approach and board slower moving commercial vessels. Once onboard, pirates typically can capture the crew and commandeer a vessel in less than 20 minutes. If the hijacked vessel is of low ransom value, such as a fishing vessel or cargo dhow, pirates may use it as a "mother ship" to launch additional attacks farther from the coast on larger, more lucrative merchant vessels.

Ransom payments are the lifeblood of Somali pirate networks, which have evolved their organized transnational criminal enterprises to include other illegal activities and expanded criminal networks. Somali pirates[1] have been paid hundreds of millions of dollars in ransom, funding more attacks and other forms of criminal activity in the region. Overall, piracy and related maritime crime in this region costs the international community billions of dollars annually.[2]

Pirate attacks emanating from Somalia are now at the lowest levels since 2006, due primarily to the following factors:

- Proactive and coordinated naval action by ships of the Combined Maritime Forces' Combined Task Force-151, NATO's OPERATION OCEAN SHIELD, and European Union Naval Forces' OPERATION ATALANTA, as well as by the national naval forces of other nations, including China, Indonesia, India, and Russia;
- Adherence by commercial vessels to industry-developed Best Management Practices[3] (BMP) and the increased use of embarked armed security teams;
- Increasing will of affected States to prosecute piracy — more than 1,400 pirates are now held in more than 20 States; and
- Improving stability in Somalia, including the creation of a new provisional constitution, new parliament, and a new presidency to support effective and responsible governance to combat the nation's social, legal, economic, and operational challenges.

Due to the success of the international community against piracy and related maritime crime off the HOA, there is the potential for the maritime industry to relax its use of BMP and to reduce overhead costs by sailing without privately contracted armed security personnel (PCASP) in High Risk Waters or by using substandard PCASP. Under the existing uneven international regulatory regime, this could result in undesirable consequences including: erosion of BMP implemented by masters, thereby increasing the likelihood of an attack; undesirable uses of force; or a successful attack by pirates against a vessel protected by substandard PCASP. Additionally, international coalitions may seek to reduce the scope and scale of counter-piracy operations as the threat appears to diminish. However, the decline in incidents does not necessarily imply a reduction in the threat to vessels transiting through the HOA. Although many of those involved in financing and leading pirate attacks have temporarily moved on to other ventures, pirate groups remain operational. Suspicious approaches continue to be reported in the Arabian Sea, the Indian Ocean, the southern Red Sea, the Gulf of Aden, and the Gulf of Oman. In addition, Somali pirates retain the capability to target vessels at great distances from the Somali coast, highlighting the importance of continued caution and the potential danger of complacency.

The basic conditions that permitted piracy to flourish in the first place – a lack of effective control by legitimate security forces of the littoral and maritime areas of Somalia, a poor economy, a lack of regional governance and corruption, and inadequate legal consequences — have improved over the last few years, but significant improvements are still required. A reduced commitment by naval counter-piracy force providers or diminished self-protection measures by commercial shipping likely will result in a resurgence of successful hijackings. There appears to be a growing awareness among Somalis themselves of the toxic effect piracy and related maritime crime has on their communities. Proactive prosecution and long prison sentences have directly challenged the impression of impunity for this crime. As a result, pirates have been pushed out of some locales along the Somali coast.

Objectives

The paramount goal of the United States is to safeguard U.S. citizens and U.S. interests, including protection of the lawful flow of commerce off the HOA. This will best be accomplished in the maritime domain by repressing Somali piracy through actions by the United States and the international community in the short term and by enabling the Somali government to eventually police its own territory. The United States, in concert with partner nations, international coalitions, and nongovernmental organizations, will continue to focus on the three primary areas of prevention, response, and governance. U.S. departments and agencies, consistent with respective authorities and other national missions and priorities, shall pursue the following objectives.

Prevention of Attacks

The international community, despite its commitment to combating piracy and related maritime crime, cannot effectively patrol the entire region off the HOA. Support by industry and merchant mariners is critical to making the pirate business model unsustainable. Making piracy and related maritime crime an untenable business is best realized by preventing the capture of merchant mariners and commercial vessels in waters under pirate threat, which will significantly hinder financial gains by the criminal enterprise. Specific actions including the following:

- **Inform U.S. citizens.** Maritime Advisories and Port Security Advisories, which clearly outline regional threats, continue to provide critical guidance on BMP to protect U.S. merchant mariners, ships, and cargo off the HOA. U.S. departments and agencies will work with public-facing elements of the United States Government, such as the Department of State's Bureau of Consular Affairs, the U.S. Coast Guard, and the Department of Transportation to provide timely threat assessments and warnings for U.S. citizens and companies traveling off the HOA.
- **Lead and participate substantively in the ongoing work of the Contact Group on Piracy off the Coast of Somalia,** which the United States helped to establish in January 2009 pursuant to U.N. Security Council Resolution 1851.
- **Encourage international commercial shipping firms to increase the compliance rate for BMP and harden vessels, including the incorporation of properly trained and equipped armed security.** Partner with the shipping industry to improve practical steps merchant ships and crews take to avoid, deter, delay, and counter pirate attacks. The shipping industry's use of BMPs and the increasing use of PCASP are among the measures that continue to be the most effective deterrents against pirate attacks.
- **Lead and participate substantively in the Maritime Security Working Group established by the Maritime Safety Committee at the International Maritime Organization (IMO)** to provide communication and education in U.S. policies and doctrines involving counter-piracy preventive measures, and to assist in the development of guidelines and recommendations to increase global participation by IMO Member States in counter piracy prevention measures.
- **Pursue the implementation of international standards for PCASP,** which include an integrated approach to security, planning, training, awareness, documentation, and communication skills.
- **Continue industry partnerships,** including organizing and participating in workshops with the maritime industry to update, educate, and share information on ways to mitigate the threat of piracy.

Respond to Acts of Maritime Crime

The United States will continue to ensure that pirates do not have easy access or freedom of action in the Indian Ocean, Red Sea, and Gulf of Aden through continued naval and law enforcement support.

- **Provide persistent interdiction-capable presence at sea off the HOA.** Consistent with other U.S. mission requirements, U.S. Navy and/or U.S. Coast Guard forces operating in the region provide persistent interdiction through presence, conduct maritime counter-piracy operations, and coordinate counter-piracy activities with other forces operating in the region to the extent practicable. When in range, these forces will prevent suspected pirate vessels from operating, respond to reports of pirate attacks with the objective of disrupting such attacks, and, in appropriate circumstances, terminate the act of piracy and any resultant hostage situation with intent to deliver any surviving pirates ashore for prosecution. These forces will also coordinate efforts among all multilateral coalitions such as Combined Maritime Forces, NATO's OPERATION OCEAN SHIELD, the European Union's OPERATION ATALANTA, and independent naval forces.
- **Reinforce the longstanding U.S. policy of discouraging the payment of ransoms, prisoner release, policy changes, or other acts of concession.** Ransom payments lead to future hijackings of ships at sea, and future hijackings lead to additional ransom payments. Such ransom payments build the capacity of militant and terrorist organizations to conduct attacks.
- **Encourage and support international counter-piracy initiatives.** The United States will leverage the efforts of various international bodies, such as the Maritime Security Centre – HOA in Northwood, United Kingdom, and the Regional Fusion and Law Enforcement Center for Safety and Security at Sea (REFLECS3) in Victoria, Seychelles, to combat piracy and related maritime crime, share information, build capacity; and Shared Awareness and Deconfliction (SHADE) meetings.
- **Disrupt and dismantle pirate bases ashore.** Pirates require land-based support and access to weapons to commit acts of violence. Piracy at sea can only be reduced if pirate bases ashore are disrupted or dismantled. U.N. Security Council resolutions confer the authority to take "all appropriate measures" to end piracy, including operations

in the littoral and land territory of Somalia. As such, the United States will work with other governments and international organizations to disrupt and dismantle pirate bases to the fullest extent permitted by U.S. and international law.

- **Employ criminal investigative capabilities to identify and target the finances of criminals who operate at the higher organizational levels of the piracy enterprise.** The piracy model is based on the economic benefits associated with crime. Targeting the finances of the organization and blocking assets of organizational leaders will assist in defeating the criminal enterprise that supports piracy and related maritime crime. The United States will continue to block the assets of certain persons determined pursuant to Executive Order 13536 to have threatened the peace, security, or stability of Somalia through acts of piracy or armed robbery at sea off the coast of Somalia.
- **Support and encourage the exercise of relevant and appropriate jurisdiction through the framework of applicable international conventions.** In addition to the relevant customary international law on piracy reflected in the 1982 Law of the Sea Convention, the 1979 Hostage Taking Convention, the 1988 Convention on the Suppression of Unlawful Acts Against the Safety of Maritime Navigation, the 2000 Transnational Organized Crime Convention, and the 1999 Terrorist Financing Convention may apply to piracy cases in some circumstances. The United States will fully support and encourage the appropriate exercise of jurisdiction over interdicted pirates in accordance with relevant international law.

Enhance Maritime Security and Governance

Defeating piracy and maritime crime in the long term requires a stable government with a regional population that supports and defends the rule of law. Pirates and those who commit maritime crime flourish under weak governance and cannot function effectively under rule of law. The United States, along with our international partners, will facilitate the development of regional governance by Somalia, including transitional support for prosecution and imprisonment of criminals.

- **Promote the re-establishment of governance, security, and economic development in Somalia through the encouragement of political and social will.** This objective will take decades, if not generations, to implement. In the meantime, our efforts to combat piracy and related maritime crime will help foster maritime trade security, regional stability, and the recovery of Somalia from two decades of civil war.

- **Facilitate, where necessary, the expeditious investigation and prosecution of suspected pirates with lawful and appropriate consequences.** It is a key deterrent to piracy and other maritime crime to prosecute individuals who commit these acts and deliver appropriate consequences when there is sufficient evidence. Releasing a suspected pirate without investigation or trial is likely to have little deterrent value for other potential pirates. Conversely, rigorous investigations and convictions with meaningful sentences will reduce the number of active pirates and deter potential recruits. Where U.S. prosecution is not appropriate, we will seek agreements and arrangements with States in the region to facilitate prosecution of suspected pirates.
- **Facilitate the development of laws and regulations of States and regional cooperative organizations to combat piracy and related maritime crime.** Encourage States, and provide assistance when necessary, to adopt domestic legislation and supporting programs that will permit the effective prosecution of those who commit, incite, or facilitate acts of piracy.
- **Develop the investigative and judicial capacities of regional nations.** Work bilaterally, and with other interested parties, to identify the nature and scope of international assistance needed to enhance the capacities of States in the region, specifically with respect to the arrest, detention, prosecution, and incarceration of persons involved in piracy and related maritime crime, including arms trafficking and money-laundering to support piracy operations. Promote and assist information-sharing efforts between and among industry, law enforcement, prosecutors, and intelligence professionals to identify and apprehend land-based facilitators in maritime piracy networks.
- **Support international and regional efforts to combat transnational organized crime.** A significant reason for the decline in piracy acts in the past several years is the African Union Mission in Somalia (AMISOM) efforts to stabilize the region. These efforts have built institutional and operational capacity, disrupted criminal networks, and degraded conditions along the Somali coast that have enabled pirates to operate.

- **Establish the regional maritime patrol capacity of Somalia in concert with other capacity-building efforts.** Developing the capacity of Somalia to guard and defend its own coast will limit the number of suitable coastal areas available to anchor hijacked ships, making piracy more difficult and less profitable. Partnering with like-minded organizations, such as the European Union's regional Maritime Security Programme (MASE), will address multiple aspects of maritime crime, including piracy, drug and weapon smuggling, human trafficking, illegal fishing, and maritime pollution.
- **Educate the Somali government and civilians on the negative effects that piracy and related maritime crime has on communities and economic growth.** A robust understanding of how the lack of governance, corruption, and illegal activity detrimentally affect the country's population will engender opposition to criminal enterprises.

Partnerships

International cooperation and integration among regional nations, international organizations, industry, and other entities that have an interest in maritime security and ensuring a full range of lawful and timely actions are necessary to combat piracy and related maritime crime off the HOA.

Most of the world's maritime domain is not subject to the sovereignty or jurisdiction of any single State, and many States do not have the capability or capacity to protect commercial shipping on the high seas, or even within their own territorial seas. International coalitions and partner nations that provide maritime patrol forces contribute to reducing, but cannot provide a complete response to, this threat. An effective response to piracy and related maritime crime requires coordinated and comprehensive multilateral and multi-sectorial cooperation on a global scale with regional focus.

Established in January 2009, the CGPCS has been a remarkably - perhaps uniquely - effective ad hoc construct that brings together stakeholders from governments, international organizations, private industry interests, and charitable, not-for-profit organizations to deliver coordinated solutions to Somali piracy.

Operating independently of, but in close coordination with, the United Nations, the CGPCS is enabled by a series of U.N. Security Council resolutions that recognize and promote its role as the primary coordinator of international efforts to counter Somali piracy. The United States will continue to lead and participate substantively in the work of the CGPCS as it advances our national objectives to combat piracy and develop sustainable efforts that, in the long term, will help to reestablish the rule of law in Somalia.

In addition to cooperation with CGPCS, the United States will continue to lead, support, and collaborate with the efforts of other international organizations including Combined Maritime Force's Coalition Task Force-151, and SHADE meetings.

Implementation, Monitoring, and Review

Successful implementation of these efforts can be measured tangibly by the trends of successful pirate attacks, BMP compliance rates by industry, the percentage of suspected pirates who are prosecuted, and increased maritime security governance and stability within the region. Consideration of intangible benefits may also be evaluated through the Maritime Security Sector Reform Guide[4] created jointly by the Departments of State, Defense, Homeland Security, Transportation, and Justice and the U.S. Agency for International Development.

The Counter-Piracy Steering Group (CPSG), consisting of a high-level interagency working group led by the Departments of State and Defense, will coordinate, implement, and monitor the objectives outlined in this Plan. The CPSG will continue to assess methods, expenditures, and agency activities to reduce risk and protect the maritime industry from piracy and related acts of maritime crime.

The Departments of State, Defense, Homeland Security, Justice, Transportation, and the Treasury, and the Director of National Intelligence will contribute to, coordinate, and undertake initiatives to support this Framework within existing resources.

The CPSG will provide recommendations to the National Security Council, through the Maritime Security Interagency Policy Committee, to update this policy when conditions in Somalia change.

United States Counter Piracy and Maritime Security Action Plan – Annex B

Framework for Combating Piracy and Enhancing Maritime Security in the Gulf of Guinea

Background

Piracy and related maritime crime in the Gulf of Guinea (GOG), a strategically significant region of Africa, are increasingly placing at risk the interests of the United States and our allies and partners. These maritime crimes threaten to undermine the four pillars of the *U.S. Strategy Toward Sub-Saharan Africa*, which include spurring broad-based and inclusive economic growth, trade, and investment, as well as advancing peace and security. Hijackings for fuel and cargo oil theft constitute the majority of incidents, though there are also significant numbers of robberies and kidnappings for ransom (KFR). These maritime attacks largely occur in weakly governed territorial seas that extend as far west as Cote d'Ivoire and as far south as Gabon.

The GOG suffers from a combination of factors that make it vulnerable to piracy, robbery at sea, and related maritime crime that are far more complex and violent than that occurring on the east coast of Africa. Many countries in the GOG region have ineffective governance, weak rule of law, precarious legal frameworks, inadequate naval, coast guard, and maritime law enforcement forces, and corrupt systems of government. While crude oil theft has been an issue for many years in the Niger Delta, recent hijackings of tankers transporting refined petroleum products and the increase in kidnappings for ransoms off the Niger Delta are of growing concern for both mariners and the oil industry operating in the region. When maritime criminals focus on the high value cargo aboard oil tankers and general cargo vessels, with little regard for the operators, it becomes much more dangerous for mariners.

Criminals can only thrive in areas where they operate with impunity either due to inadequate criminal justice systems or governments that are susceptible to corruption. For many people in the GOG, including the most powerful individuals, illicit markets present opportunities for personal enrichment not found in the legal economy with low risk of negative consequences.

Partnerships with politically committed stakeholders, like the Economic Communities of West and Central African States, are critical to reducing opportunities for maritime crime and piracy within the GOG. Nigeria has the largest regional economy, and its potential willingness to institute rule of law and effective governance will reflect much of what can be achieved by the entire region.

The maritime sector is fundamental to a State's national defense, law enforcement, economy, and social goals and objectives. Africa's seas, lakes, and rivers are crucial sources of livelihood, as well as food and water security for many communities. These water sources also serve as a platform for trade and commerce (including for landlocked countries), as a theater for potential conflict, and, if poorly governed, as an area that transnational criminal networks can exploit with impunity. Investors are less inclined to do business in risky environments due to the increased cost of operating in higher crime areas. The absence of effective maritime governance dissuades capital investment, discourages growth, threatens food security, and hinders a State's ability to improve the conditions that contribute to its citizens' quality of life. This leads to increases in other areas of maritime crime, such as illegal, unreported, and unregulated fishing; human trafficking; the smuggling of narcotics; and circumventing sanctions through the shipment of contraband goods and weapons. In contrast, improved levels of maritime security enable a State to more effectively detect, deter, and interdict illicit actors whose actions indirectly or directly challenge local governance, health, and stability. Improvements in governance promote stability and encourage the growth of commerce within those nations that enforce rule of law.

The United States and partner nations play a leading role in western Africa's oil sector, which provides high-quality, light-sweet oil, and is important to the region's economy. Nigeria, Gabon, Ghana, and other countries around the GOG produce more than 3 million barrels of oil a day, or about one-third of Africa's output. Nigeria and Equatorial Guinea are also leading liquefied natural gas exporters. Oil output disruptions in West Africa could affect global oil prices, including within the United States, due to strong interconnectedness within the international market. Seafarers are becoming increasingly wary of using the seas in the GOG as the number of acts of piracy, armed robbery at sea, and related maritime crime rises. The United States must continue to partner with member states in the GOG to increase maritime security capacity, forge a concerted effort to stem piracy and armed robbery at sea, and prevent the region from becoming susceptible to the same conditions associated with the Horn of Africa.

The foundation for expanding maritime security in the GOG exists within strategies recently developed by African nations. The 2050 African Integrated Maritime Strategy (2050 AIMS), which was adopted at the 22nd Annual African Union (AU) Summit in January 2014, provides member States with many ambitious goals, including a regional vision that establishes a “Blue Economy”[1] in African waters before 2050. West and Central African nations signed a Code of Conduct[2] in Yaoundé in June 2013 that will be instrumental in enforcing maritime law. The International Maritime Organization (IMO) also supports the efforts of Economic Community of Central African States (ECCAS) and the Economic Community of West African States (ECOWAS) in its strategy, *Implementing Sustainable Maritime Security Measures in West and Central Africa.*

Overview of the Threat

Maritime crimes targeting high-value asset operations in the GOG emerged as a regional problem in the late 1990s. Since then, the incidence of piracy and armed robbery at sea in the GOG has waxed and waned, but has remained a concern for the shipping and energy industries, as well as for regional states and their trading partners. As of 2014, armed criminals, primarily based out of Nigeria, generally steal cargoes consisting of refined oil or other products. Unlike piracy off the Horn of Africa, the Nigerian criminals have no safe place to keep captured ships while negotiating ransoms. Generally speaking, there are three types of incidents in the GOG– low-level robberies, kidnap for ransoms, and hijacking for cargo theft. Although most attacks continue to happen inside territorial seas, many attacks occur beyond 12 nautical miles and often beyond the range of navies in the region. The overall number of attacks remains very difficult to gauge because incidents often go unreported. The attacks damage Nigeria’s lucrative oil industry as the hijackings of product tankers increase the risk of doing business in the country. Estimates indicate that the country is losing approximately $1.5 billion a month to maritime crime, which includes piracy, armed robbery at sea, smuggling, and bunkering fraud, and its production is 400,000 barrels below its capacity of 2.5 million barrels per day.

Criminal groups that conduct KFR in Nigeria typically target small tug and supply vessels, and these groups are likely operating separately and independently from the fuel-theft networks likely based in Lagos. All of the reported KFR incidents around the GOG have occurred off the Niger Delta region.

In the GOG, maritime criminals are able to take advantage of a well-established illicit and corrupt political economy, as well as a lack of consistent and effective governance in the maritime domain. Criminals in this region maintain access to established international criminal networks and close ties to the shipping industries. Consequently, attacks are better coordinated than off the Horn of Africa, executed with precision, and often impossible to trace. West Africa's criminal organizations have deep international ties, and the trends indicate an increased willingness for criminal gangs to venture further from their shore-side bases to commit their crimes.

On average, there are 12 to 15 GOG port calls a year by U.S.-flagged, deep draft cargo ships. Approximately 70 U.S.-registered Offshore Supply Vessels (OSVs) are working out of Nigerian and Ghanaian ports supporting offshore oil exploration. Both types of vessels carry crews that may include U.S. citizens. In addition, there are numerous vessels operating in the GOG and engaged in coastwise trade, which requires operating in territorial seas and coastal waters and making frequent port calls in the region. An unknown number of U.S. mariners work aboard these vessels, as well as on cargo ships, tankers, and OSVs flagged in other nations operating in the region. The escalation in violent criminal activities will increasingly put U.S. citizens in harm's way and has already required the expenditure of significant resources to resolve hostage situations.

The pattern of piracy and related maritime crime also raises an increasing concern due to the violence associated with hijackings. In its 2014 report on piracy and armed robbery at sea, the International Maritime Bureau warns of the dangers to ships transiting West African waters, particularly around Nigeria, Benin, and Togo, and urges heightened vigilance, drawing particular attention to the expansion of the danger region. In 2013, the number of Nigerian criminal maritime attacks grew and currently stands at its highest level since 2008. Nigerian criminals accounted for 31 of the 51 attacks reported in the region in 2013, and West Africa, as a whole, saw 19 percent of attacks worldwide last year. The increase in maritime attacks in West Africa led London-based Lloyd's Market Association, an umbrella group of maritime insurers, to list Nigeria, Benin, and nearby waters in the same risk category as Somalia. The result was a significant decrease in maritime traffic in the region, which led to a substantial loss in revenue for regional nations and significant impact on the livelihoods of the country's citizens through an increase in the cost of imports and a decrease in the competitiveness of exports.

The nature of the attacks, porous borders, limited maritime law enforcement and interdiction assets, endemic corruption, and lack of political will allow criminal gangs to carry out fast attacks with the ability to quickly return to shore and avoid detection and capture. In addition, a high number of attacks are widely believed to be unreported due to an ongoing failure by regional States to pursue criminal action, complicity by law enforcement officials, and a desire to keep insurance rates low.

Objectives

The paramount goal of the United States is to safeguard U.S. citizens and U.S. interests, including protecting the lawful flow of commerce in the GOG. This will best be accomplished in the maritime domain by reducing corruption, increasing the political will, and developing the capacity and coordination of regional maritime authorities in the GOG to patrol and monitor illicit activity effectively and provide sufficient protection of vessels conducting lawful commerce. Although the underfunding of the maritime sector by regional states will present near-term challenges, a continued focus on the link between economic development and maritime security provides the best prospect for a sustainable approach. The United States, in concert with partner nations, international coalitions, and nongovernmental organizations, will continue to focus on the three primary areas of prevention, response, and governance. U.S. departments and agencies, consistent with respective authorities and other national missions and priorities, will pursue the following objectives.

Prevention of Attacks

The regional community, despite its efforts to increase coordination and capacity, is not yet able to patrol the entire region in the GOG effectively. Actions by industry and merchant mariners are critical in protecting cargo and preventing the capture of merchant mariners and commercial vessels in high-risk waters. Techniques to hinder and prevent maritime criminals continue to be the best method for increasing security and safety of mariners.

- **Inform U.S. citizens.** Maritime Advisories and Port Security Advisories, which clearly outline regional threats, continue to provide critical guidance on best management practices to protect U.S. merchant mariners, ships, and cargo in the GOG. U.S. departments and agencies will work with public-facing elements of the United

States Government, such as the Department of State's Bureau of Consular Affairs, the U.S. Coast Guard, and the Department of Transportation, to provide timely threat assessments and warnings for U.S. citizens and companies traveling through or working in the GOG.

- **Increase the risk to criminals operating in the maritime domain.** Develop ECCAS-ECOWAS best practices to increase the consequences for criminals attempting attacks. Promote an increase in regional naval and law enforcement presence in the region to serve as a strong deterrent and quick response to maritime attacks.
- **Seek industry partnership.** The United States Government will continue to engage the shipping industry to provide input, follow best management practices, and require U.S.- flagged vessels to implement effective measures to protect against pirates and armed robbers operating at sea.
- **Track Privately Contracted Armed Security Personnel (PCASP).** The Department of State, in coordination with other interagency partners, will continue to track the regional States' procedures or restrictions for the use of PCASP in order to be able to provide current information for U.S. shipping interests.
- **Pursue the implementation of international standards for PCASP,** which include an integrated approach to security, planning, training, awareness, documentation, and communication skills. GOG nations have strongly resisted including PCASP within their territorial seas. The United States and maritime partners must respect the sovereignty of these nations, while also demonstrating the benefits of well-trained PCASP in increasing maritime security and lawful commerce.
- **Assist in the development of enhanced regional maritime patrols.** Although GOG States prohibit, to varying degrees, the use of PCASP (including the import and export of weapons and equipment), there remains a need for enhanced security in these more dangerous territorial seas. Within the territorial seas of GOG nations, the marine industry must rely on the maritime security capabilities of the regional States. Most of these nations often lack resources and trained personnel; in addition, corrupt officials may be complicit in and actively encouraging maritime attacks. To protect mariners, the United States should promote - and assist in strengthening - the concept of armed convoys and/or regional maritime patrols to increase sustainability and effectiveness.

Respond to Acts of Maritime Crime

Building on the successful efforts against piracy and armed robbery at sea, the United States will continue to provide naval and law enforcement presence when available, and build capacity with regional nations to combat maritime crimes and facilitate lawful commerce within the GOG. Enhanced capabilities will strengthen partner nations' capacities to exercise their authorities and responsibilities to deter, detect, and interdict unlawful acts, such as the illicit movement of people, drugs, arms, and money. Increased capacity also enables governments to support other at-sea governance concerns including the ability to provide assistance to preserve the safety of life at sea and address the welfare of maritime migrants, including refugees and asylum seekers.

- **Strengthen regional maritime capacity.** The GOG will continue to be a priority area for U.S. security assistance. U.S. maritime-sector assistance should be provided in a multi-national setting with other international partners, when possible, and focused on regional engagement built on strong partnerships with key countries. The United States Government trains, equips, and conducts exercises and operations with African maritime forces through programs like Africa Partnership Station, which is conducted cooperatively with our international partners. The United States should investigate providing excess defense articles to nations that have the capacity to absorb increased capability and demonstrate resolve and commitment to countering piracy and related maritime crime. The United States will reinforce the importance of port security, as a key component of maritime security, and provide advice on implementing all aspects of the International Ship and Port Facility Security Code.
- **Expand combined operations with African partners.** The primary reason U.S. warships are operating in the region is to support capacity-building efforts. Consistent with other U.S. mission requirements and priorities, the United States should continue to conduct the African Maritime Law Enforcement Partnership (AMLEP) mission. A valuable partnership and capability building mechanism, AMLEP focuses on partner nation jurisdiction and criminal justice sector capability to identify areas where additional capacity building would strengthen the entire interdiction and enforcement continuum. AMLEP has contributed significantly to establishing more effective maritime security operations off the coasts of Senegal, The Gambia, and Cabo Verde. Many of the lessons

learned in these nations can be applied throughout the GOG. Ghana, Togo, Benin, and Nigeria are priority countries for future AMLEP expansion, followed by Cameroon, Gabon, Cote d'Ivoire, and Sao Tome and Principe.

- **Reinforce the longstanding U.S. policy of discouraging the payment of ransom, prisoner release, policy changes, or other acts of concession.** The payment of ransom emboldens criminal enterprises and does little to deter future acts of piracy or kidnapping.
- **Facilitate the development of an integrated strategy among all GOG nations to enhance intelligence and information sharing, training, assets, surveillance, and maintenance, and increase their ability to control waters.** The development of shared maritime domain awareness, including both enhanced capability and operational coordination mechanisms, pursuant to a regional framework, will increase synergy and transparency in combating piracy, armed robbery at sea, and related maritime crime.
- **Support the development of operational planning by key countries, such as Nigeria, Ghana, and Cameroon.** The efficient use of available resources, such as placing patrol boats at key strategic chokepoints and conducting random boardings, will inhibit kidnappers and other organized criminals from deploying from, and returning to, safe havens. The United States will support efforts by Nigeria to enforce land-based security in the Niger Delta and reduce strongholds for maritime criminals.
- **Lead regional operations and training exercises, in coordination with international partners, to develop competencies with regional navies and coast guards.** Several nations in the region, which have limited maritime crime in their territorial seas, possess great potential to share lessons learned through successful training programs and capable interdiction operations. The United States and international partners should expand naval security training (focusing on anti-piracy), including tracking, interdicting, seizing, and prosecuting criminals.
- **Encourage nations to implement the Code of Conduct3 and pursue regional integration.** Critical progress can be made in the development of domestic laws and regulations that criminalize piracy and related maritime crime, coupled with joint maritime interdiction operations and enhanced judicial systems.

- **Develop regional capability to conduct law enforcement investigations.** Analysis of crime scenes following piracy and violent attacks, including the collection of forensic evidence and case package development, will increase the success of pursuing and prosecuting leaders of criminal enterprises.

Enhance Maritime Security and Governance

Defeating piracy and related maritime crime requires functional governments with the political will to pursue and prosecute all levels within criminal enterprises. Maritime crime flourishes under complicit governance and is limited under effective rule of law. Absent strong commitment and action from local governments, there is little reason to believe that attacks in the GOG will decline. Therefore, the United States, along with our international partners, will advise and facilitate the development of regional governance, enhance political will to combat these crimes, develop key institutions to prosecute perpetrators, and support increased economic development.

- **Strengthen the judicial sector.** This includes strengthening the broad array of civil and criminal justice-related activities required to support rule of law and compliance in the maritime domain. In addition to the relevant customary international law on piracy reflected in the 1982 Law of the Sea Convention, the 1979 Hostage Taking Convention, the 1988 Convention on the Suppression of Unlawful Acts Against the Safety of Maritime Navigation, the 2000 Transnational Organized Crime Convention, and the 1999 Terrorist Financing Convention may apply to piracy cases in some circumstances. We will fully support and encourage the appropriate exercise of jurisdiction over interdicted pirates in accordance with relevant international law.
- **Build political will and strategic frameworks.** The United States will continue to support ECCAS and ECOWAS in their effort to develop regional frameworks for maritime cooperation. The United States has supported the organizations and its member states in drafting the signed ECCAS-ECOWAS Memorandum of Understanding and a Code of Conduct for Central and West Africa. Further support will be necessary in supporting the regional bodies and member states in their effort to draft and execute an implementation plan for the frameworks. The United States should also continue its support to ECOWAS and member States on their

effort to implement the ECOWAS Integrated Maritime Strategy and establish a pilot maritime Zone E (Nigeria, Benin, Togo, and Niger).

- **Strengthen information sharing.** The United States Government will encourage and support the Maritime Trade Information Sharing Center – Gulf of Guinea (MTISC-GOG) in Accra, Ghana. The MTISC-GOG aims to improve the regional maritime domain picture, analyze the information received, and share the information with regional maritime operations centers and industry vessels and production facilities in the GOG. Additionally, U.S. support to regional and national maritime operation centers will facilitate greater information sharing and improve operational standards.
- **Support the capacity of States' in the region to address the impunity for those actors conducting or facilitating piracy and related maritime crime.** The GOG Code of Conduct includes a commitment from signatory States to ensure persons committing or attempting to commit a transnational crime in the maritime domain are apprehended and prosecuted. Where appropriate, the United States Government will help our African partners build their capacity to investigate and prosecute cases effectively. Two potential focus areas are the States' ability to collect forensics evidence from the ships after an attack, and coordination among law enforcement, navies, and prosecutors.
- **Promote sustainable, broad-based, and inclusive maritime economic development.** Inequitable distribution of benefits from marine resources – such as fisheries, minerals, oil, and gas – poses serious threats to peace and security in Africa. Inclusive economic growth will ensure that benefits are broadly distributed in an open, transparent, and participatory approach. The United States will focus on improving: science-based decisionmaking processes; integration of human-built and natural infrastructure to maintain ecosystem goods and services upon which many vulnerable coastal communities depend; maintenance of critical habitats for cost-effective coastal adaption and resilience; a modern marine transportation system; and support for capacity building and regulatory focus for sustainable management of maritime revenue streams from tourism, fishing, resource extraction, commercial shipping, and port operations. The United States Government will continue to encourage Nigerian government representatives to work closely with civil society to address systemic problems related to maritime security.

- **Strengthen the Africa Constituency.** Additional efforts to develop an Africa constituency will support and enable stakeholders (coastal communities, civil society, private sector, academic, media, commerce, scientific, etc.) to engage in the decision-making process over marine resource use, benefit equitably from these resources and maritime commerce, access reliable data and information as it relates to maritime issues, and generate a demand for strong maritime security.
- **Promote accountable, transparent, and responsive governance.** The United States will support and empower key reformers and institutions of government at all levels to promote the rule of law; strengthen checks on executive power; incorporate responsive governance practices; enhance transparent accounting of oil-related sales; transfers, and investments; develop policies to strengthen maritime security; and improve decision-making processes at national and local levels, including specific maritime, commercial, regulatory, and/or criminal justice institutions. The United States also will emphasize to key nations that complicity in oil theft leads to increased instability and reduced profits for the entire nation.
- **Use strategic communications to maintain political momentum and action by the African regional organizations and their member states.** The United States Government will seek bilateral and multilateral opportunities to emphasize the need for good maritime governance and action to hold individuals accountable for acts of piracy and related maritime crime.

Partnerships

International cooperation and integration among regional nations, international organizations, industry, and other entities that have an interest in maritime security is necessary to ensure the full range of lawful and timely actions to combat piracy and related maritime crime in the GOG.

Most of the world's maritime domain is not subject to the sovereignty or jurisdiction of any single State, and many States do not have the capability or capacity to protect commercial shipping on the high seas, or even within their own territorial seas. International coalitions and partner nations that provide maritime patrol forces contribute to reducing, but cannot provide a complete response to, this threat. An effective response to piracy and armed robbery at sea requires coordinated and comprehensive multilateral and multi-sectorial cooperation on a global scale with regional focus.

Cooperation in the GOG between the coastal regional governments occurs through ECOWAS and ECCAS. U.N. Security Council Resolutions 2018 (2011) and 2039 (2012) noted that States in the region have a leadership role to play and the international community should assist in strengthening their efforts. This was supported in August 2013 when the U.N. Security Council released a presidential statement recognizing "the primary responsibility of [regional] States in the eradication of piracy and armed robbery at sea." Although the political will and regional cooperation are limited within the GOG, nations have the capability to govern and control their territorial seas.

Established in 2013, and as an outcome of the U.S.-hosted November 2012 G-8++ Africa Clearinghouse, the G-8++ Friends of Gulf of Guinea (FOGG) serves as the primary international coordination body on GOG maritime security. The FOGG meets on a biannual basis with a focus on donor coordination to improve the collective goal of sustainable capacity building. Participation to date has included the AU, Australia, Belgium, Brazil, Canada, Denmark, ECOWAS, ECCAS, the European Union, France, Germany, Interpol, Italy, Japan, the Netherlands, Norway, Portugal, Russia, Spain, the United Kingdom, the United Nations Office of Drugs and Crime (UNODC), and the United States. The United States actively participates in the G-8++ FOGG. The first G-8++ FOGG meeting in the GOG region was held in November 2013.

We continue to work with our international partners to strengthen collective lines of effort. Working in coordination with France and the United Kingdom, the United States developed a G-8++ matrix to help coordinate international activities in the region, which is based on the U.S. Maritime Security Sector Reform Guide. The United States is also leading an effort, in coordination with the United Kingdom, France, the European Union, UNODC, and Interpol, to develop a joint strategy to address impunity of those who commit acts of piracy and related maritime crime in the GOG by focusing on the elements necessary for States to prosecute the criminals effectively.

Industry, a primary contributor to the development of the economy in the region, plays a large role in partnerships against piracy and related maritime crime. As a key component in the economic engine, independent oil companies should be encouraged to partner with nations that support transparency and cultivate responsibility in promoting safety and security at sea. Industry will naturally increase investments where risk remains low.

The United States should continue to partner with industry to support maritime law enforcement efforts.

Implementation, Monitoring, and Review

A strategic milestone will be the development of an implementation plan for the GOG Code of Conduct by the African partners. The operationalization of Zone E by Togo, Benin, and Nigeria will also demonstrate the level of political will and capacity to regionalize the African response to the piracy and armed robbery threat. An increase in investigating and prosecuting cases and a reduction in the trend of piracy and related maritime crime will also serve as a tangible indicator of successful implementation of this Plan. Consideration of intangible benefits may also be evaluated through the Maritime Security Sector Reform Guide created jointly by the Departments of State, Defense, Homeland Security, Transportation, and Justice and the U.S. Agency for International Development.

The Counter Piracy Steering Group (CPSG), consisting of a high-level interagency working group led by the Departments of State and Defense, will coordinate, implement, and monitor the objectives outlined in this Plan. The CPSG shall continue to assess methods and agency activities to reduce risk and protect the maritime industry from acts of piracy and related maritime crime.

The Departments of State, Defense, Commerce, Energy, Homeland Security, Justice, Transportation, and the Treasury, and the U.S. Agency for International Development and the Director of National Intelligence will contribute to, coordinate, and undertake initiatives in support of this Framework within existing resources. United States Government departments and agencies will coordinate activities, design sustainable solutions to maritime security based on a comprehensive and multi-dimensional approach, and support, as feasible, African-led and owned maritime security initiatives. The CPSG will provide recommendations to the National Security Council, through the Maritime Security Interagency Policy Committee, to update this policy when conditions in the GOG change.

End Notes

[1] PPD-18 Maritime Security, August 14, 2012, which reaffirms the 2005 National Strategy on Maritime Security and establishes issue-related Maritime Frameworks, one of which is piracy off the Horn of Africa.

[2] National Security Council Countering Piracy off the Horn of Africa: Partnership & Action Plan, December 2008.

[3] National Strategy on Maritime Security, 2005.

[4] Policy for the Repression of Piracy and other Criminal Acts of Violence at Sea, June 2007.

[5] Id

[6] International Outreach and Coordination Strategy, November 2005.

End Notes for Annex A

[1] http://oceansbeyondpiracy.org/sites/default/files/documents old/The Economic Cost of Piracy Full Report.pdf.

[2] Ibid.

[3] Best Management Practices for Protection Against Somalia Based Piracy, Version 4 printed August 2011, ISBN: 978 1 85609 5051.

[4] http://www.marad.dot.gov/documents/Maritime_Security_Sector_Reform.

End Notes for Annex B

[1] The 2050 AIMS defines "Blue Economy" as an approach that "improves African citizens well-being while significantly reducing marine environmental risks as well as ecological and biodiversity deficiencies."

[2] Code of Conduct Concerning the Repression of Piracy, Armed Robbery Against Ships, and Illicit Maritime Activity in West and Central Africa, 2013.

[3] Code of Conduct Concerning the Repression of Piracy, Armed Robbery Against Ships, and Illicit Maritime Activity in West and Central Africa, 2013.

In: U.S. Maritime Counterpiracy Efforts
Editor: Gilles Hornes
ISBN: 978-1-63463-334-5

Chapter 3

PIRACY OFF THE HORN OF AFRICA*

Lauren Ploch, Christopher M. Blanchard, Ronald O'Rourke, R. Chuck Mason and Rawle O. King

SUMMARY

Pirate attacks in the waters off Somalia and the Horn of Africa, including those on U.S.-flagged vessels, have brought renewed international attention to the long-standing problem of maritime piracy. According to the International Maritime Bureau (IMB), at least 219 attacks occurred in the region in 2010, with 49 successful hijackings. Somali pirates have attacked ships in the Gulf of Aden, along Somalia's eastern coastline, and outward into the Indian Ocean. Using increasingly sophisticated tactics, these pirates now operate as far east as the Maldives in good weather, and as far south as the Mozambique Channel. Hostage taking for ransom has been a hallmark of Somali piracy, and the IMB reports that more hostages, over 1,180, were taken at sea in 2010 than any year since records began; over 86% of those were taken by Somali pirates.

The increase in pirate attacks off the Horn of Africa is directly linked to continuing insecurity and the absence of the rule of law in war-torn Somalia. The absence of a functioning central government there provides freedom of action for pirates and remains the single greatest challenge to regional security. The lack of law enforcement capacity creates a haven

* This is an edited, reformatted and augmented version of a Congressional Research Service publication, No. R40528, dated April 27, 2011.

where pirates hold hostages during ransom negotiations that can last for months. Some allege that the absence of Somali coastal security authorities has allowed illegal international fishing and maritime dumping to go unchecked, which in turn has undermined coastal communities' economic prospects, providing economic or political motivation to some pirates. The apparent motive of most pirate groups, however, is profit, and piracy has proven to be lucrative. Somalia's "pirate economy" has grown substantially in the past two years, with ransoms now averaging more than $5 million. These revenues may further exacerbate the ongoing conflict and undermine regional security.

The annual cost of piracy to the global economy ranges between $7 and $12 billion, by some estimates. The U.N. Security Council has issued a series of resolutions since 2008 to facilitate an international response, which is coordinated by a multilateral Contact Group. The Council has authorized international navies to counter piracy both in Somali territorial waters and ashore, with the consent of Somalia's Transitional Federal Government (TFG), and has also authorized, as an exemption to the U.N. arms embargo on Somalia, support for the TFG security forces.

Counter-piracy patrols by multinational naval forces near Somalia are intended to compliment mariners' self-protection measures. Increased patrols and proactive efforts by ships have reduced attacks in the Gulf of Aden, but the U.N. Secretary-General warns that "while the effectiveness of naval disruption operations has increased and more pirates have been arrested and prosecuted, this has not stopped piracy. The trend of the increased levels of violence employed by the pirates as well as their expanding reach is disconcerting." Some suggest that a perception of impunity exists among pirates and financiers; nine out of ten Somali pirates apprehended by naval patrols are reportedly released because no jurisdiction is prepared to prosecute them.

The United States has sought to prevent, disrupt, and prosecute Somali piracy through a range of interagency and multilateral coordination and enforcement mechanisms. The Obama Administration has initiated a new "dual track" policy toward Somalia, where some contend that international efforts to build a credible central authority have failed. Congress has examined options to address piracy both diplomatically and militarily. Congress appropriates funding and provides oversight for policy initiatives with implications for piracy in the region, including maritime security assistance to regional governments, support to peacekeeping operations in Somalia, and funding for U.S. Navy operations. Congress continues to debate options for addressing pirate safe havens and improving the prospects for prosecution of pirate suspects.

RECENT DEVELOPMENTS

Despite international naval efforts to counter acts of piracy in the waters off Somalia, pirates in this region continue to increase not only the sophistication and geographic range of their attacks, but also the level of violence against hostages. Hostages are also being detained longer, as pirates hold out for ransom payments that now reportedly average over $5 million per ship. Heightened military presence in an internationally recommended transit corridor in the Gulf of Aden has reduced attacks in that area, but pirates have adopted tactics that now allow them to attack more than 1,000 nautical miles off the Somali coast.

Pirate attacks in the Gulf of Aden, the Red Sea, and the waters far off Somalia's eastern coast, including the Arabian Sea, have been attributed to Somali pirates. The number of attacks in this area, which had roughly doubled annually from 2007 to 2009, rising from 51 reported attacks to 217, appeared to level off in 2010, when 219 attacks were reported.[1] Attacks in the Gulf of Aden declined by more than half in 2010, attributed in large part to international naval patrols. Attacks east and south of Somalia, however, increased substantially, up from 19 reported attacks in 2008 and 80 in 2009 to over 140 in 2010. As of March 2011, Somali pirates had been sighted as far east as off the coast of India, and as far south as the Mozambique Channel. The two monsoon seasons in the Indian Ocean appear to dampen pirate activity in these waters, but, with the end of the winter monsoons, the spring months of 2011 have corresponded to a spike in attacks.[2]

The International Maritime Bureau (IMB) reports that, in 2010, over 1,016 crew members on dozens of hijacked vessels were taken hostage by Somali pirates. Most were released following ransom negotiations, but at least 13 were injured and eight killed. In the first three months of 2011, IMB data indicates that almost 100 vessels in the region reported being attacked, with 15 successful hijackings involving approximately 300 hostages. These attacks represent a substantial increase from the same period last year, when 35 vessels were attacked in the waters off Somalia. At least seven hostages have been killed to date in 2011, including four Americans. As of April 2011, Somali pirates were holding over 26 ships and 530 crew hostage while seeking ransoms.

Attacks on U.S. Vessels

U.S. ships represent a small but high profile percentage of those attacked by Somali pirates.[3] In March 2011, the *Maersk Alabama*, which had been the target of a widely reported attack in 2009 and an unsuccessful attempt in 2010, was approached by suspected pirates for a third time. The *Alabama*, which now has armed security guards onboard, deterred the pirates with defensive manoeuvres. Two U.S. warships were attacked by Somali pirates in 2010.

The deaths of four Americans on February 22, 2011, onboard the sailboat *Quest* mark the first known American casualties during a Somali pirate attack. The *Quest* had been hijacked less than 200 nautical miles off the coast of Oman four days prior, and the pirates were reportedly in the process of taking it back to an anchorage off the Somali coast when they were intercepted by four U.S. Navy vessels, including an aircraft carrier, a guided missile cruiser, and two destroyers. Details surrounding the incident remain under investigation, but, according to U.S. Navy reports, pirates onboard the *Quest* fired a rocked-propelled grenade (RPG) at one of the destroyers, the *U.S.S. Sterrett*, after negotiations broke down with two pirates who had boarded the *Sterrett* for talks with a Federal Bureau of Investigation (FBI) hostage negotiator. A Navy SEAL team subsequently boarded the *Quest* and found that the American hostages had been shot and fatally wounded. Some Somali accounts differ with the Navy account, claiming that the hostages were caught in crossfire during a rescue attempt by the SEALs. Two pirates were found dead onboard, and two others were killed during the raid. The remainder, 13 Somalis and one Yemeni, were captured and brought to Norfolk, Virginia, where have been indicted by a grand jury. An additional indictment was issued in March for Mohammad Saaili Shibin, who is accused of serving in a leadership role as the pirate gang's hostage negotiator. Shibin, who reportedly earned $30,000 for his negotiating role in the 2010 hijacking of a chemical tanker, was apprehended in Somalia in a joint operation by Somali security forces and the FBI in April.[4] He is the first piracy suspect captured onshore in Somalia to be tried in the United States. Another suspected pirate negotiator, Ali Mohamed Ali, was arrested at Dulles International Airport on April 21, 2011, in relation to the 2008 hijacking of a Danish vessel carrying American cargo (see below).

To date, U.S. courts have tried Somali pirates from three other incidents.[5] In November 2010, five Somalis involved in the April 2010 attack on the U.S. Naval frigate *U.S.S. Nicholas* were the first to be convicted of piracy by a U.S. jury since 1820. They were given life sentences plus 80 years for related firearms charges by a civilian court in Norfolk, Virginia in March 2011. A Somali involved in the 2009 hijacking of the *Maersk Alabama*, Abduwali Abdiqadir Muse, was sentenced by a New York court in February 2011 to almost 34 years in prison on charges of hijacking, kidnapping, and hostage taking. Muse was not convicted of piracy. A federal judge dismissed piracy charges against six Somalis implicated in the April 2010 attack against another warship, the *U.S.S. Ashland*, in August 2010. One of the defendants, Jama Idle Ibrahim, pled guilty to related charges and to conspiracy to commit piracy in a 2008 attack on a Danish ship carrying American cargo. Ibrahim, who reportedly received a $17,000 share of a $1.7 million ransom for the Danish vessel, is now serving a 30-year term for both crimes.[6] The remaining five face seven other charges; prosecutors have appealed the decision to dismiss the piracy charge.

U.S. and International Efforts to Prevent Pirate Attacks

The U.S. government and the international community have undertaken an array of efforts to prevent and deter pirate attacks. Various authorities have issued warnings to vessels in the waters off the Horn of Africa and continue to provide guidance on measures to maximize their safety while transiting the area.[7] In addition to an existing advisory warning to U.S. vessels regarding the threat of piracy in the waters off the Horn issued by the U.S. Department of Transportation Maritime Administration (MARAD),[8] the U.S. Coast Guard has, in the wake of the *Quest* attack, issued a warning strongly advising all U.S. registered yachts and sailing vessels against passage in the Gulf of Aden, Arabian Sea, Somali Basin, and western parts of the Indian Ocean. These vessels are particularly vulnerable to attack because of their low speed and low freeboard (the height of a ship's deck above the water level). The shipping industry, in coordination with the combined naval forces conducting counter-piracy operations, has produced guidance, known as *Best Management Practices* (BMPs), for mariners transiting these high risk waters.[9]

The U.S. Navy continues to conduct counter-piracy operations in the region, primarily through the Combined Task Force 151 and NATO's Operation Ocean Shield. The European Union and NATO have extended the mandates for their counter-piracy missions through the end of 2012. China and Russia have assisted EU forces in escorting World Food Program relief shipments and China has shown willingness to improve its cooperation with the coalition task force providing security escorts in the Maritime Security Patrol Area in the Gulf of Aden.

International coordination of anti-piracy efforts has improved over the past two years, both at sea and in the region, but U.S. civilian and military officials continue to stress the importance and difficulty of finding solutions to the problem of instability ashore in Somalia. To that end, the African Union (AU) has extended the mandate of their peacekeeping force in the country, the African Union Mission to Somalia (AMISOM). In December 2010, the U.N. Security Council passed Resolution 1964, extending its approval of AMISOM's mandate through September 2011 and raising the troop level to 12,000. The United States had provided training, logistics support, and assistance worth over $365 million to AMISOM.[10] The United States has also provided over $85 million in assistance to the Somali Transitional Federal Government (TFG) security forces. AMISOM and TFG forces continue to face attacks from Al Shabaab, an Islamist insurgent group with ties to Al Qaeda. Capacity building efforts for these forces have focused on stabilizing Mogadishu before extending beyond the capital, and the TFG has yet to demonstrate the ability to expand its authority along the coast. Further complicating the security situation is a growing debate about the TFG's legitimacy as its mandate approaches expiration in August 2011.[11]

U.N. Secretary-General Ban Ki-moon released his latest report on piracy off Somalia to the Security Council in October 2010.[12] He reported that ships following "best practices" developed by the maritime industry had a significantly lower risk of being hijacked. The Secretary-General also reported on the situation in Somalia in December 2010 and gave an update on international anti-piracy efforts.[13] He has noted a request from the TFG President for support to develop Somalia's security forces and train its coast guards as part of international efforts to address piracy. The African Union has called on the Security Council to approach the Somali piracy issue "in a holistic manner, with the view to effectively addressing its underlying causes and other equally serious threats which affect the livelihood and well-being of the Somali people."

The situation in Somalia, and the related piracy threat, was the subject of open debate at the Security Council in March 2011, during which the Council stressed the need for a "comprehensive strategy to encourage the establishment of peace and stability in Somalia," and a "comprehensive response to tackle piracy and its underlying causes." Among the items on the Council's agenda was a report issued in January by the Secretary-General's Special Advisor on Legal Issues Related to Piracy off the Coast of Somalia.[14] The Special Advisor has proposed, among other recommendations, the creation of three specialized piracy courts for Somalia to address current obstacles to the prosecution of Somali pirates. The Security Council expressed unanimous support for increased efforts to establish governance and the rule of law in Somalia in Resolution 1976, passed on April 11, noting concern with the large number of suspected pirates being released without trial and deciding to urgently consider the establishment of the specialized Somali courts recommended in the Special Advisor's report (see "Prosecuting Acts of Piracy").

BACKGROUND

Piracy has reemerged as a global security threat, most recently in the waters off the Horn of Africa, but also in West Africa, the waters off India, the South China Sea and the Strait of Malacca, and the Caribbean. Pirates tend to operate in regions with large coastal areas, high levels of commercial activity, small national naval forces, and weak regional security cooperation mechanisms. These characteristics facilitate other maritime security threats, including terrorism, weapons and narcotics trafficking, illegal fishing and dumping, and human smuggling operations.

Worldwide rates of piracy began to increase in the early 1990s, peaking at roughly 350 to 450 reported attacks per year during the period 2000-2004, then declining by almost half by 2005. In 2007, almost half of the world's reported pirate attacks took place in African waters, mainly near Nigeria and Somalia. The number of attacks in Somali waters doubled in 2008, accounting for an estimated 40% of the 293 pirate attacks reported worldwide.[15] The recent increase in pirate attacks off Somalia has caused the total number of worldwide pirate attacks to return to the levels of 2000-2004: of the 406 worldwide attacks in 2009, 217 of them occurred off the coast of Somalia. In 2010, 219 of the 445 reported attacks took place in the waters off the Horn. Moreover, high-profile attacks on high-value vessels in the Gulf of Aden and the west Indian Ocean have brought renewed international attention to the problem of piracy in these waters.

The U.S. National Maritime Security Strategy, issued in 2005, stated that the "safety and economic security of the United States depends upon the secure use of the world's oceans," and identified "well organized and well equipped" pirates and criminals as threats to international maritime security. The bombing of the *U.S.S. Cole* in 2000 in the Yemeni harbor of Aden and the bombing of the French oil tanker *MV Limburg* in 2002 illustrated the threat of potential maritime terrorism in the region. The United States, working with international partners, established a combined naval task force to meet the terrorism threat (Combined Task Force 150), and increased bilateral military assistance to regional navies. However, prior to the establishment in January 2009 of the new Combined Task Force 151, the United States had not assigned any naval assets the sole task of performing anti-piracy operations in the Horn of Africa region.

Similarly, until 2008, the international community did not respond to the threat of piracy in the waters off of Somalia in a coordinated, dedicated manner. In December 2008, the European Union launched EU NAVFOR Operation ATALANTA, the first naval operation under the framework of the European Security and Defense Policy (ESDP). Similarly, NATO launched a dedicated anti-piracy mission, Operation Ocean Shield, and other navies have deployed ships to provide security for vessels bearing their flags. The development of a collaborative regional response in East Africa in 2009 mirrored regional reactions to the threat of piracy in the Strait of Malacca between Malaysia, Singapore and Indonesia, which are credited with having drastically reduced the instance of piracy in Southeast Asia since 2005. Eradicating piracy off the Horn of Africa region may prove to be a more daunting task. The vast areas of the west Indian Ocean and the Gulf of Aden where the pirates operate are remote, Somalia remains largely ungoverned, and regional states have relatively weak naval capabilities. Furthermore, Somalia's transitional government currently lacks the capacity to prosecute and imprison pirates and few countries have demonstrated the will to prosecute those apprehended in international counter-piracy operations.

Piracy off the Horn of Africa: Profile

The Pirates

Several pirate groups currently operate in Somali waters, according to U.N. and independent sources.[16] Initially organized predominantly along clan lines and based in remote port towns, the groups have varying capabilities and patterns of operation, making generalized responses more difficult. Reports suggest that there may currently be 7 to 10 distinct gangs or "pirate action groups" financed by so-called "instigators" who organize the funding and delegate operations to group leaders.[17] These groups operate from Xabo on Puntland's northern coast, along Puntland's eastern coast out of ports from Garacad (Garad) south to Hobyo, and from Harardhere (Xarardheere) in central Somalia south to Kismayo.[18] U.N. officials have expressed particular concern with a "recent and worrying trend," since September 2010, regarding attacks launched between Harardhere and Kismayo, a region currently occupied by militants affiliated with Al Shabaab.[19] U.S. officials state that "interactions mostly of a coercive nature that benefit terrorists" exist, but do not appear to represent an "operational or organizational alignment."[20]

Pirate groups have operated from many of these remote communities, each heavily dependent on fishing, since the early 1990s. Several of the early pirate groups adopted names to suggest that they were acting in a maritime security capacity, claiming that they had been trained by foreign security firms and given semi-official status to intercept foreign fishing vessels and extract fines.

In recent years, though, piracy appears to have become an attractive pursuit for young Somali men with few other economic prospects, adding legal complexities for governments seeking to try young pirate suspects. Pirate groups are also reportedly recruiting from inland Somalia.

Puntland

The northern semi-autonomous region of Puntland (shaded in Figure 1) continues to serve as the primary base for Somali pirate networks, and some local officials there are alleged to have facilitated and profited from piracy, in spite of some recent efforts by regional leaders to crack down on pirate activity and related corruption. In March 2010, the U.N. Monitoring Group on Somalia reported that key leaders in the Puntland administration "have received proceeds from piracy and/or kidnapping," and, that "in some cases the Puntland authorities have extended protection to pirate militias."[21] Puntland authorities protested the report's conclusions and characterized them as politically motivated. The TFG and the Puntland authorities agreed in 2009 to a joint program for anti-piracy cooperation, and, later that year, the Secretary-General reported that local Puntland authorities had "succeeded in launching limited relevant activities to thwart, curb, or investigate piracy."[22] Puntland's efforts to push pirates out of their base in Eyl were reportedly successful, although those pirates appear to have simply moved their operations south to Garacad. Puntland and the TFG signed a memorandum of understanding on counter-piracy issues in April 2010, although the Puntland government suspended engagement with the TFG in January 2011, apparently spurred by a perceived lack of consultation by the TFG with regional authorities on the future of the transitional government.[23] Puntland has developed a basic coast guard, but accounts suggest that the equipment and capabilities of this small force remain limited. The government has enlisted a private security company to train and equip its maritime force.

Motives

While the profitability of piracy appears to be the primary motivating factor for most pirates, other observers argue that since conditions in Somalia make survival difficult for many and prosperity elusive for most, the relative risk of engagement in piracy seems diminished.[24] According to the final report of the experts group convened in 2008 by the U.N. Special Representative to Somalia, "poverty, lack of employment, environmental hardship, pitifully low incomes, reduction of pastoralist and maritime resources due to drought and illegal fishing and a volatile security and political situation all contribute to the rise and continuance of piracy in Somalia."[25] Pirate activity and ransom revenues have increased significantly in the past three years, and many now assert that Somalia's economy and its population are increasingly dependent on piracy. The average ransom paid in 2010 has been estimated at over $5.4 million—with more than 50 reported hijackings in the last year, this places the pirates' 2010 ransom revenues at over $250 million.[26] U.N. officials argue that the insecurity caused by piracy deprives northern Somalia, which has not been as affected by the armed conflict in central and southern Somalia, of a variety of job-creating investments, from port operations to commercial fishing.

Somali pirates interviewed by the international media frequently link their pirate activities to trends such as illegal fishing and dumping in Somali waters that have emerged as the country has lost its ability to patrol its waters over time.[27] While these explanations may mask the opportunistic piracy of some, reports suggest that illegal fishing and dumping have disrupted Somalia's coastal economy. Recent estimates by the United Nations suggest that Somalia may lose $95 million annually to illegal fishing.[28] The international Contact Group on Piracy off the Coast of Somalia (CGPCS, see below) stated at its inaugural meeting that "piracy is symptomatic of the overall situation in Somalia including the prevalence of illegal fishing and toxic waste dumping off the coast of Somalia, which adversely affects the Somali economy and marine environment."[29] The CGPCS also reaffirmed "its respect for Somalia's sovereignty, territorial integrity, and sovereign rights over natural resources" and underscored that the group's participants "ensure that their flagged vessels respect these rights."

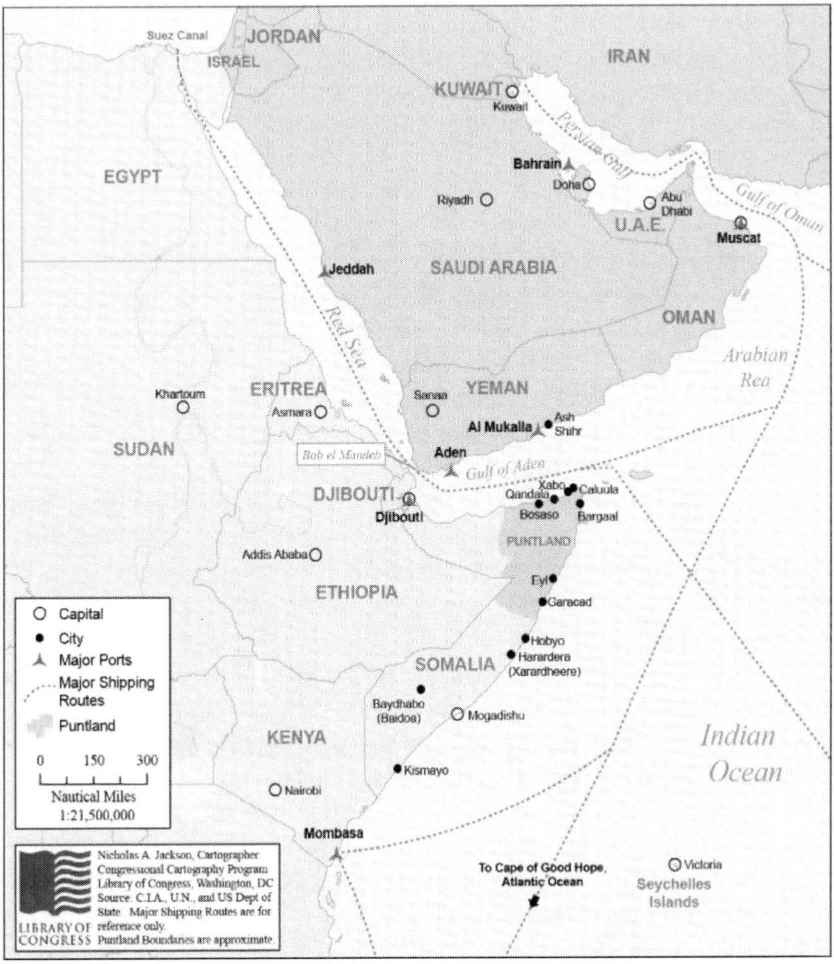

Source: Congressional Cartography Program, Library of Congress, adapted by CRS Graphics.

Figure 1. The Horn of Africa, Surrounding Waters, and Key Locations.

Paradoxically, the regional fishing industry reportedly has been damaged significantly by the threat of piracy. According to some reports, tuna catches in the Indian Ocean fell 30% in 2008, in part because of fishing vessels' fears of piracy. This has had a major impact on countries like the Seychelles, which rely on the fishing industry for up to 40% of their revenues, and on Yemen, which reported an estimated $150 million in lost fishing sector revenues in 2009.[30]

Tactics and Demands[31]

As noted above, some Somali pirate groups have developed sophisticated operational capabilities and have acquired weaponry, equipment, and funds that make them on par with or more effective than the local forces arrayed against them. The typical Somali pirate team is equipped with a variety of small arms, including AK-47 rifles and rocket propelled grenade (RPG) launchers. Many pirate teams use fishing skiffs powered with large outboard motors to give chase to larger, but slower moving tankers, cargo ships, yachts, cruise ships, barges, and tug boats. Local Somali fisherman reportedly are forced to support pirate activities in some cases, while in other cases, coastal Somalis lend their fishing boats, equipment, and navigational expertise to teams of would-be pirates from inland communities.

Somali pirates initially focused on attacking ships in the west Indian Ocean, off Somalia's eastern coast. When ships operating on that route shifted further out to sea, Somali pirates shifted their focus to the Gulf of Aden, where there is a concentration of merchant ships (an estimated 33,000 per year)[32] operating in a more constrained waterway that is relatively close to Somalia's northern shore. Most recently, now that international naval forces are patrolling the Gulf of Aden with some effectiveness, Somali pirates have shifted some of their focus back to the Indian Ocean, and are now able to operate over 1,000 nautical miles from the Somali coastline, often with the support of so-called 'mother ships.' These 'mother ships' are usually larger fishing vessels that have been commandeered through acts of piracy.

As noted above, U.S. and international officials suspect that in some cases, Somali businessmen and international support networks provide pirate groups with financing and supplies in return for shares of ransom payments that are also distributed among pirates themselves.[33] The IMB has disputed claims that pirates receive intelligence support in order to target specific vessels, arguing that "the suggestion that vessels are targeted in advance using shore based intelligence is spurious.... Further, there is no information in the public domain that would enable pirates to precisely locate a targeted vessel at sea and then to mount a successful attack off the Horn of Africa."[34] In March 2010, the U.S. Office of Naval Intelligence (ONI) reported that "vessels attacked off Somalia are randomly selected and not specifically targeted for any reason other than how easily the vessel can be boarded. Pirates simply patrol an area, wait for a target of opportunity, and attempt to board."[35] The pirates refuel and purchase logistical supplies like engine parts in Yemen, according to U.S. naval officials.[36]

One of the unique characteristics of Somali piracy has been the taking of hostages for ransom. In this sense, piracy off Somalia can be viewed as a form of maritime kidnapping. Unlike pirate attacks in Strait of Malacca or Nigeria, where ships are boarded either to take the vessel or its contents, pirates off the Horn of Africa routinely take the target vessel's crew hostage in return for ransom payments. This approach to piracy is possible because the pirates have a sanctuary on land in Somalia and in its territorial waters from which they can launch pirate attacks and hold hijacked ships for indefinite lengths of time during ransom negotiations. Pirates in other parts of the world are less likely to have such sanctuaries. This has presented maritime security forces with significant challenges to traditional engagement strategies and tactics.

According to reports, most vessels under attack have less than 15 to 30 minutes between the first sighting of the pirates and their boarding of the ship and taking of hostages. If a naval ship cannot arrive on scene within those 15 to 30 minutes, it will likely arrive too late to prevent the ship's capture. Naval combatant ships generally can steam at speeds of up to 30 knots (speeds of 20+ knots might be more likely), so unless a naval ship happens to be a few miles away when a commercial ship comes under attack, it won't arrive until after (perhaps long after) the 15- to 30- minute window has come and gone. The large area of water to be patrolled and the relatively small number of naval ships available means that the closest naval ship is often far too distant to arrive within that timeframe.

Once a ship is taken, the pirates will generally move the ship to an anchorage off the Somali coast. Hostages may be kept on their own vessel, moved to a larger vessel with other hostages to discourage rescue attempts and consolidate hostage "upkeep," or they may be taken ashore. Negotiations for ransom involve the use of satellite telephones, third-party intermediaries in Somalia and abroad, and public relations efforts to influence interaction with property owners and foreign officials. As ransom payments have increased, however, so has the length of ransom negotiations, which on average doubled from 2009 to 2010.[37] Hostages may now face three to four months of captivity, or, in the case of Paul and Rachel Chandler, a British couple whose sailboat was seized in October 2009, over a year before being released. Hostages held by Somali pirates have reported harsh conditions and psychological trauma endured during captivity.

Ransom v. Rescue: Considerations Regarding the Use of Force

While pirate attacks may involve violence and the use of weaponry, reports suggest that most Somali pirate groups have not wantonly harmed captives taken in the course of their raids.[38] Somali pirates have, however, demonstrated an increasing willingness to use violence in order to capture a ship, and, according to the commander in charge of EU counter-piracy operations, their treatment of hostages appears to be worsening.[39] According to the U.S. Office of Naval Intelligence (ONI), the number of vessels fired upon by Somali pirates in 2009 (127) and 2010 (120) was triple the number fired upon during 2008 (42).[40] Pirates appear to be adapting to certain self-defense mechanisms used by mariners, and have, in some instances, used RPGs or explosives to breach a ship's "citadel" (a safe room with a reinforced door used by crew to avoid capture).

Most navies have avoided rescue operations that could endanger the lives of hostages, preferring instead to engage in hostage negotiations or wait for shipping companies to negotiate ransom. Several high profile rescue attempts have led pirates to threaten revenge.[41] Pirate groups have threatened to kill hostages in the event of such attempts. Hostages may also inadvertently be caught in the crossfire during rescue operations. In April 2009, a rescue operation by French naval forces designed to free a family held hostage onboard a small sailboat off the Somali coast resulted in the death of the vessel's owner, a French citizen, during an exchange of fire between the pirates and naval personnel.[42] In January 2011, South Korean commandos successfully rescued the crew of the tanker *Samho Jewelry*, but the tanker's captain was shot in the stomach during the operation. The deaths of four Americans onboard the *Quest* in February 2011 further highlights the dangers to hostages while being held by pirates.

The use of force against suspected pirate vessels also may be problematic because of the difficulty inherent in distinguishing a pirate mother ship from a legitimate commercial ship. According to reports, in November 2008, a ship from the Indian navy attacked what it thought was a pirate mother ship; only after the attack did the navy discover that the targeted ship was an innocent Thai commercial trawler.

Ransoms Paid to Somali Pirates

Some of the most sensational cases of piracy have been resolved through the payment of large sums of money to different pirate syndicates. The Ukrainian ship *Faina* was released for a reported $3.2 million ransom in February 2009 after being held for nearly 6 months by pirates based in Harardhere.

> The seizure of the ship, carrying T-72 tanks and a significant amount of ammunition and small arms, led several governments, including the United States, to dispatch naval forces to the region to monitor the ship and its cargo. The Saudi oil supertanker *Sirius Star* was released for a reported $3 million ransom to Eyl-based pirates in January 2009 following its seizure in November 2008. Media reports suggested Somali pirates received a $4 million ransom in December 2009 to release the Chinese bulk coal carrier *MV De Xin Hai,* and $7 million to release the Greek supertanker Maran Centaurus. The highest known ransom paid to date is $9.5 million, for the release of the South Korea oil tanker *Samho Dream* in November 2010.

Ransom payments are considered to be problematic because they encourage pirates to continue their attacks with the expectation that insurance and shipping companies will decide that ransoms are cost effective relative to the insured values of personnel and cargo. Reports suggest that pirates have invested ransom earnings in more sophisticated weaponry and have fortified their operating bases against local authorities and potential international intervention. With pirate revenues in 2009 estimated at roughly $80 million, local authorities like the governments of Puntland and Somaliland are completely out-resourced.[43]

Piracy off the Horn of Africa: Impact

The strategic location of the Horn of Africa increases its importance for international security and commerce. The northern coastline of Somalia lies to the south of the Gulf of Aden, a key transit zone for ships passing to and from the Red Sea and the increasingly active port of Djibouti. The U.S Department of Energy estimates that 3.2 million barrels of oil per day transited the Bab el Mandeb strait between the Gulf of Aden and the Red Sea in 2009.[44] The Indian Ocean waters off the southeast coast of Somalia are home to busy shipping lanes for trade between Asia and East Africa, as well as for ships making longer voyages around South Africa's Cape of Good Hope. Ship traffic to and from the Kenyan port of Mombasa is particularly vulnerable to security disruptions in the west Indian Ocean. The Maritime Administration testified in 2009 that:

> On average, at least one U.S. commercial vessel transits the area each day. Many of these US-flag vessels carry Department of Defense cargo bound for Operations Iraqi and Enduring Freedom. U.S.-flag vessels transiting the region also carry humanitarian cargoes generated by U.S. AID or international organizations to the Horn of Africa, including Djibouti, Somalia and other countries in East Africa or South Asia.[45]

A recent study conducted by the One Earth Future Foundation estimates that maritime piracy costs the international community between $7 and $12 billion per year.[46] As the study notes, the threat of pirate attacks in the region inflicts direct costs, including insurance, ransoms, self-protection measures, rerouting, naval operations, and piracy prosecutions. Piracy also imposes secondary costs, having a macroeconomic impact on regional trade, on the region's tourism and fishing industries, and on food prices.

Threats to Commercial Shipping and Global Trade[47]

Piracy results in several types of economic costs to the shipping industry, including ransom payments, damage to ships and cargoes, delays in cargo deliveries, increased maritime insurance rates, and costs to harden merchant ships against attack. Some of these costs are ultimately passed on to the consumer. The total economic costs of piracy, though large in an absolute sense, are nevertheless only a small fraction of the total value of worldwide shipborne commerce.

In May 2008, based on the advice of the Lloyd's Joint War Committee, insurance underwriters at Lloyds of London designated the Gulf of Aden a "war-risk" zone subject to a special insurance premium. In response, London-based ocean marine insurers raised premium rates for ships making the voyage through the Gulf of Aden and the Suez Canal. War risk insurance premiums charged by international reinsurers have also increased dramatically for vessels sailing in the danger zone.[48] Depending upon the vessel size, war risk premium for merchant vessels sailing in the Indian Ocean has reportedly gone up from $500 per ship, per voyage, to up to $150,000 per ship, per voyage.[49]

American shipping companies would have faced the same insurance cost pressures were it not for the fact that American hull clauses exclude piracy, which is then picked up under the U.S. Maritime War Risk Insurance Program. U.S. hull and machinery rates have been relatively stable due to the U.S. Maritime War Risk Insurance Program, the competitive nature of the ocean marine insurance business, U.S. naval patrols off the Horn of Africa, and actions taken by owners to protect their ships and cargo. Moreover, according to representatives of the American Institute of Marine Underwriters (AIMU),

U.S. ocean marine insurers have not had to pay ransom for any act of piracy; therefore, they say, hull and cargo insurance rates for vessels leaving the United States remain relatively stable.

London-based shipping firms are usually prepared to pay ransom when the demanded sums are considered low, ranging from $500,000 to $2 million, compared with the value of the ships and cargo. Prior to 2009, such payments were reportedly reimbursed because hull insurance policies[50] issued in London explicitly covered the peril of piracy.[51] American hull clauses exclude piracy, which is then picked up by the war risk clause. However, when the ransom demanded exceeds the value of the cargo, the shippers typically do not pay the ransom. Some firms have developed specific insurance products to address piracy-related ransom costs.[52]

In 2009, as the frequency of vessel seizures and ransom demands in the Gulf of Aden and Indian Ocean spiked to unprecedented levels, some marine underwriters in London began to shift from covering piracy under hull policies to covering the peril under war risk policies.[53] This change may have been taken in an effort to address possible ambiguity in how piracy (including marine kidnap and ransom) is covered. The purchase of a war risk policy obviates the need for a separate marine kidnap and ransom insurance policy. Under the hull policy, the kidnap and ransom perils are generally covered under a contractual provision called "general averages" whereby the owner, insurance company, and other interested parties enter into an agreement prior to each shipment to pay a proportional share of a vessel's expenses in the event of piracy that may or may not include kidnap and ransom. The problem is that in the event of an actual piracy certain ambiguities and legal challenges arise.

Some ship operators (and their governments) reportedly judge the costs of paying occasional ransoms to be far less than the costs of rerouting the shipping around the southern tip of Africa— a longer and more costly trip—or arming merchant ships. Some experts argue the payment of ransoms in the event of vessel seizure has kept the level of violence associated with piracy relatively low. Thus, the payment of occasional ransoms might be viewed by ship operators (and their governments) as a regrettable but tolerable cost of doing business, even if it encourages more piracy. According to the State Department, "continued payments will only encourage more kidnappings. For this reason, the United States actively encourages other states to adopt our no concessions policy and refrain from paying ransoms."[54]

Threats to Humanitarian Aid Deliveries

Piracy also threatens the delivery of vital humanitarian assistance to the Horn of Africa, much of which arrives by sea.[55] According to the U.S. Agency for International Development (USAID), more than 5 million Ethiopians will require emergency food assistance through mid-2011. The United States provided over $340 million in food and humanitarian aid to Ethiopia in FY2009, over $363 million in FY2010, and over $22 million in the first half of FY2011.[56] In neighboring Somalia, an estimated 2.4 million people, one-third of the population, are expected to require food aid in 2011, primarily in southern and central Somalia, where poor rains have resulted in crop failure and deteriorating livestock conditions. The delivery of U.S. food and humanitarian aid to Somalia is additionally hindered by a non-permissive security environment on land.

Food insecurity in the region, caused by drought and instability, has been heightened by high food and fuel prices in the region. Officials from the World Food Program (WFP), which ships tens of thousands of metric tons of food monthly to the Horn of Africa region, reports that it has become more expensive to ship assistance to Mogadishu, and that their ability to deliver relief is significantly hampered. Al Shabaab militants demanded in December 2009 that the WFP halt imports of food assistance in favor of purchasing supplies from Somali farmers. The WFP suspended operations in southern Somalia in January 2010, amid growing threats and intimidation. Canada, NATO, and European Union forces assumed escort responsibilities for WFP shipments in late 2008. Russia has also escorted convoys. In March 2010, China's navy offered to assist the European Union forces currently escorting WFP shipments, signaling the expansion of China's naval deployment to the region.

Threats to U.S. Flagged Vessels and the Maersk Alabama Incident

The threat of piracy to ongoing relief efforts and U.S.-flagged vessels was illustrated in April 2009, when pirates hijacked the *Maersk Alabama* and attacked the *Liberty Sun*, both U.S.-flagged and crewed cargo vessels contracted by WFP to deliver USAID food assistance off the southeast coast of Somalia. On April 8, 2009, Somali pirates seized the U.S.-flagged commercial shipping vessel *Maersk Alabama* approximately 250 nautical miles south east of the Somali town of Eyl. The *Maersk Alabama* had delivered food aid to the port of Djibouti and was en route to the port of Mombasa, Kenya, when it was seized by Somali pirates. Press reports suggested that the 20- member crew of U.S. citizens overtook their Somali captors sometime after the ship was seized and attempted unsuccessfully to free the ship's captain, Vermont resident Richard Phillips.

In response, the United States Navy dispatched the *U.S.S. Bainbridge*,[57] an Arleigh Burke-class destroyer, and reconnaissance aircraft to the area in order to monitor the small craft where Captain Phillips was being held. FBI personnel conducted hostage negotiations for his release. On April 11, after officials determined that Phillips' life was in immediate danger, U.S. Special Forces mounted a rescue operation with the authorization of President Obama. Three pirates were killed by snipers in the operation; a fourth, a young Somali named Abdiwali Abdiqadir Muse, was transferred to the United States for trial. [58] He pled not guilty to piracy, conspiracy, hostage taking, and weapons charges before the United States District Court in the Southern District of New York, but was convicted and, in February 2011, sentenced to 34 years in prison.

Some analysts expressed concern that the rescue operation would trigger the use of increasingly violent tactics by pirates. A leader of the pirate group that had held Phillips reportedly vowed revenge, telling reporters that, "this matter will lead to retaliation and we will hunt down particularly American citizens travelling our waters. Next time we get American citizens ... they [should] expect no mercy from us." An April 14, 2009 attack on a second U.S.-flagged vessel, the *Liberty Sun*, appeared to be an attempt by pirates to follow through on that threat. A pirate leader told reporters after the *Liberty Sun* attack that, "We were not after a ransom. We also assigned a team with special equipment to chase and destroy any ship flying the American flag in retaliation for the brutal killing of our friends."[59] The *Maersk Alabama* has come under attack twice since the first attack, but has successfully repelled pirates using an armed security team, evasive manoeuvres, and long range acoustic devices.

Concerns Regarding the Financing of Regional Conflict and Terrorism

The volatile Horn of Africa is home to several ongoing armed conflicts, and armed banditry is a common threat in much of the region. The small arms trade in the Horn and its potential to fuel instability remains a major concern to the international community. In spite of the longstanding U.N. arms embargo on Somalia established by Security Council Resolution 733 (1992), U.N. observers have reported "persistent violations." The embargo was modified in 2007 at the behest of the African Union and others to allow the armament of transitional government forces battling Islamist insurgents, and again in 2008 to allow for counter-piracy operations (see "United Nations Security Council" below). According to the Security Council Resolution 1851, "the lack of enforcement of the arms embargo ... has permitted ready access to the arms and ammunition used by the pirates and driven in part the phenomenal growth in piracy."

Some observers have expressed apprehension that some of the revenue from ransoms paid for the release of ships and hostages is being used to finance an influx of weapons to the area for pirates or others. According to some experts, boats used for pirate attacks are also occasionally used to carry refugees and economic migrants from Somalia to Yemen, and some return carrying arms.[60] In 2009, U.S. Navy officials reported to Congress that they had not found financial ties between fighters associated with *Al Shabaab* and Somali pirate gangs, but that there was the potential for personnel linkages.[61] A Canadian intelligence assessment released in December 2009 reportedly described an "Islamist extremism-piracy nexus" in which Al Shabaab personnel supplied "weapons, combat training and local protection" to pirates in southern Somalia in exchange for a portion of the spoils from hijackings either in cash or seized weapons and materiel.[62]

More recent U.N. reporting has suggested that while Al Shabaab does not appear to have formed any formal alliances with pirate gangs, "local complicities have been noted," including ad hoc agreements in which some local Al Shabaab leaders permit select gangs to operate bases in central and southern Somalia in return for a portion of ransom money.[63] According to some press reports, Al Shabaab militants have reportedly demanded a 20% share of ransom payments from a Harardhere pirate gang.[64] U.S. officials testified before Congress in March 2011 that "interactions mostly of a coercive nature that benefit terrorists" exist, but do not appear to represent an "operational or organizational alignment" between the pirates and Al Shabaab.[65] To the extent that ransom payments and new arms may further empower criminal pirate groups or local militants, the challenge that such groups pose to Somali authorities could grow.

U.S. AND INTERNATIONAL POLICY RESPONSES

Piracy in the waters off the Horn of Africa is a symptom of the wider instability that has plagued Somalia and the region since the early 1990s. The internationally recognized Transitional Federal Government (TFG) has struggled in recent years to form a functional unity government and to reconstitute national security and law enforcement entities. The United States has supported reconciliation efforts in Somalia and has taken a leadership role in coordinating diplomatic and military responses to the threat of piracy in the region, in coordination with the United Nations Security Council. International donors have pledged funds for Somalia that are intended in part to support the development of security forces by the TFG, with the aim of improving local authorities' ability to act against pirates ashore. Some caution, however, that assistance and equipment provided to TFG forces may in some cases be transferred to insurgents.[66] International donors have also supported efforts by countries in the region to prosecute and imprison pirates.

To date, U.S. and international efforts to respond to the threat of piracy have taken on a multifaceted approach. In order to provide a short term response to the immediate threat to international navigation in the region's waters, the U.N. Security Council has authorized third party governments to conduct anti-piracy operations in Somali territorial waters and ashore, but only with authorization from and in coordination with the TFG. Among CTF-151, the EU's Operation ATALANTA, NATO's Operation Ocean Shield, and other navies' "national escort" operations, roughly 3 dozen combatant ships are patrolling in the region. Attacks continue in both the west Indian Ocean and the Gulf of Aden, in spite of increased international maritime security efforts in those waters, but the number of attacks in the Gulf of Aden has diminished significantly since 2009. Regional bodies such as the African Union, the Arab League, and ad hoc groupings have held consultative meetings and issued policy statements condemning piracy in the region and providing guidance for the development of coordinated, collaborative regional responses.

U.S. Policy

The U.S. National Maritime Security Strategy, issued in 2005, stated that the "safety and economic security of the United States depends upon the secure use of the world's oceans," and identified "well organized and well equipped" pirates and criminals as threats to international maritime security. In June 2007, the Bush Administration adopted a Policy for the Repression of Piracy and other Criminal Acts of Violence at Sea that stated that it is the policy of the United States to "continue to lead and support international efforts to repress piracy and other acts of violence against maritime navigation and urge other states to take decisive action both individually and through international efforts." In December 2008, the Bush Administration issued an implementation plan based on that policy to address piracy threats in the Horn of Africa region. The U.S. National Security Council's (NSC) "*Countering Piracy off the Horn of Africa: Partnership and Action Plan*" set out the objective "to repress this piracy as effectively as possible in the interests of the global economy, freedom of navigation, Somalia, and the regional states."[67] In pursuit of that objective, the plan outlined three "lines of action" for U.S. policy:

> 1) prevent pirate attacks by reducing the vulnerability of the maritime domain to piracy; 2) disrupt acts of piracy consistent with international law and the rights and responsibilities of coastal and flag States; and 3) ensure that those who commit acts of piracy are held accountable for their actions by facilitating the prosecution of suspected pirates by flag, victim and coastal States, and, in appropriate cases, the United States.

In support of the 2007 policy and 2008 plan, the Bush Administration formed an interagency Counter-Piracy Steering Group that "addresses the full spectrum of anti- and counter-piracy efforts, from piracy prevention to interruption and termination of acts of piracy, to ensure the accountability of pirates." The State Department and Defense Department are the co-leaders of the steering group and work with other U.S. government agencies, such as USAID and the Departments of Transportation, Homeland Security, Treasury, and Justice, to coordinate U.S. policies and engagement in the multilateral initiatives that have been developed since mid-2008. To date, the steering group has overseen efforts to implement elements of the December 2008 NSC *Action Plan*, which pledged U.S. support for the establishment of the international Contact Group on piracy (established January 2009, see "Contact Group on Piracy off the Coast of Somalia") and a regional counter-piracy coordination center (under development, see "The International Maritime Organization (IMO) and the Djibouti Code of Conduct").

The Obama Administration endorsed the Bush Administration's overarching strategic approach with regard to the piracy threat, and over the course of 2009, Administration officials outlined new implementation plans. In addition to providing expanded material assistance to the Somali Transitional Federal Government to support its efforts to provide security ashore, U.S. officials and military personnel have engaged leaders and officials from the regions of Puntland and Somaliland to encourage them to take action against piracy and to improve coordination with international efforts. The United States remains a leading participant in the multilateral CGPCS, and has supported the "New York Declaration" initiative to establish benchmark best practices for governments, shipping companies, and insurance firms related to maritime security and piracy.[68]

The December 2008 *Action Plan* called for U.S. "bilateral assistance programs for judicial capacity building efforts" for regional states. The Administration welcomed the September 2009 establishment of a trust fund to support regional prosecutions, and has provided some bilateral assistance to Kenya to support its prosecution efforts.[69] Comments from officials suggest the Obama Administration shares the view expressed in the *Action Plan* that U.S. anti-piracy efforts are intended "to be mutually supportive of longer-term initiatives aimed at establishing governance, rule of law, security, and economic development in Somalia."[70] This approach is also echoed in the Obama Administration's recently released Maritime Security Sector Reform (MSSR, December 2010) guide, which provides a framework for planning and assessing interagency assistance programs in the maritime security domain.[71]

A September 2010 GAO assessment of current implementation of the *Action Plan* and the Obama Administration's wider counter-piracy strategy concluded that "the effectiveness of U.S. resources applied to counter-piracy is unclear because the interagency group responsible for monitoring the Action Plan's implementation has not tracked the cost of U.S. activities—such as operating ships and aircraft and prosecuting suspected pirates—nor systematically evaluated the relative benefits or effectiveness of the Action Plan's tasks."[72] The report also warned that "agencies have made less progress on several key efforts that involve multiple agencies--such as those to address piracy through strategic communications, disrupt pirate finances, and hold pirates accountable." As described below, these efforts were identified as priorities by the United States and its international partners during 2010, and are now the focus of U.S. and multilateral efforts alongside continuing military operations.

President Obama signed Executive Order 13536 on April 12, 2010, determining that acts of piracy or armed robbery at sea off the coast of Somalia constitute an unusual and extraordinary threat to the national security and foreign policy of the United States. The order authorizes the Treasury Department, in coordination with the State Department, to identify and to block the property and interests under U.S. jurisdiction of individuals threatening the peace and security of Somalia, those obstructing the delivery of humanitarian assistance to or in Somalia, and those directly or indirectly supporting military activities in Somalia. Listed among the individuals identified in the Annex to E.O. 13536 are: Abshir Abdullahi "Boyah," described as a key organizer, recruiter, financier, and commander of a maritime militia of pirates in the Eyl area; and Mohamed Abdi Garaad, described as a principal organizer and financier of pirate activities. Garaad is identified as having acknowledged responsibility for multiple attacks, including those on the *Maersk Alabama* and the *Liberty Sun*.

United Nations Security Council

The U.N. Security Council has issued a series of resolutions since 2008 to facilitate an international response to Somali piracy. Resolution 1816 (June 2008) authorizes states acting in cooperation with, and with prior notification of, the TFG to "enter the territorial waters of Somalia for the purpose of repressing acts of piracy and armed robbery at sea" and to "use, within the territorial waters of Somalia, in a manner consistent with action permitted on the high seas with respect to piracy under relevant international law, all necessary means to repress acts of piracy and armed robbery." Resolution 1838, adopted in October 2008, calls on states with military capabilities in the region to contribute to anti-piracy efforts and clarified the standing of the authorization contained in Resolution 1816 with respect to international law.

At the request of the TFG, the mandate established in Resolution 1816 was extended for one year in December 2008 in Resolution 1846. Later that month, Resolution 1851 expanded the mandate by authorizing states and regional organizations that are acting at the TFG's request to "undertake all necessary measures that are appropriate *in Somalia* [italics added] for the purpose of suppressing acts of piracy and armed robbery at sea." Both resolutions require any authorized international measures to be undertaken in accordance with humanitarian and human rights laws. Other provisions of Resolution 1851 have guided developments since December 2008 and may inform future U.S. or international initiatives. Resolutions 1897 and 1950 extended the mandates in Resolutions 1846 and 1851 through 2010 and 2011.

Resolution 1846 also authorized the provision of technical assistance to TFG personnel and forces "to enhance the capacity of these States to ensure coastal and maritime security" in accordance with procedures outlined in Resolution 1772. Under paragraphs 11 and 12 of Resolution 1772, the supply of technical assistance to Somali "security sector institutions" was authorized, upon prior case-by-case notification to the U.N. sanctions committee for Somalia.[73] Resolution 1851 provided similar authorization to weapons and military equipment destined for the sole use of Member States and regional organizations undertaking authorized anti-piracy operations in Somali waters.

The African Union and the TFG had long requested that the broader U.N. arms embargo be amended or lifted in order to improve the capabilities of forces fighting Islamist insurgents, and in May 2009, the Security Council unanimously adopted Resolution 1872, granting new authorization for members states to participate in the training and equipping of the TFG security forces in accordance with Resolution 1772.

The U.N. Security Council has also adopted resolutions to facilitate the prosecution of Somali pirates. Resolution 1897 (December 2009) encouraged states to undertake agreements that would allow governments to embark law enforcement officials aboard coalition anti-piracy vessels for the purpose of facilitating the investigation, detention, and eventual prosecution of piracy suspects. Resolution 1918 (April 2010) required the Secretary-General to report on "possible options to further the aim of prosecuting and imprisoning persons responsible for acts of piracy and armed robbery at sea off the coast of Somalia." The Secretary-General's report, issued in July 2010, identified seven options, six of which would require finding new host sites for prosecution and imprisonment of piracy suspects.[74] The other option emphasizes increased capacity building assistance for regional governments, which is ongoing.

Overall, the report concluded that "assisting Somalia and its regions in the longer term to develop the capacity to prosecute and imprison to international standards will be essential in sustaining results in the fight against impunity for those responsible for acts of piracy and armed robbery at sea." In August 2010, the U.N. Secretary-General appointed Jack Lang as his Special Advisor on legal issues related to piracy off the coast of Somalia. Lang issued his report in January 2011, and in April, the Security Council expressed unanimous support for increased efforts to establish governance and the rule of law in Somalia in Resolution 1976, deciding to urgently consider the establishment of the specialized Somali courts recommended in Lang's report.

Legal Instruments for the Prosecution of Piracy

Several United Nations instruments address the problem of piracy, including the Convention on the High Seas, the Convention on the Law of the Sea (UNCLOS), and the Convention for the Suppression of Unlawful Acts against the Safety of Maritime Navigation (SUA Convention).[75] The United States is a signatory to the Convention on the High Seas and the SUA Convention, but not to UNCLOS.

A "global diplomatic effort to regulate and write rules for all ocean areas, all uses of the seas and all of its resources" resulted in the convening of The Third United Nations Conference on the Sea in 1973 and the adoption of UNCLOS in 1982.[76] UNCLOS generally incorporates the rules of international law codified in the Convention on the High Seas, but also comprehensively addresses the use of other areas of the sea including, for example, the territorial seas, natural resources, and the seabed.

The Convention on the High Seas, to which the United States is a party, and UNCLOS both address piracy by stating that "[a]ll states shall cooperate to the fullest possible extent in the repression of piracy on the high seas or in any other place outside the jurisdiction of any State."[77] The term "piracy" is defined in UNCLOS (Article 101) as:

(a) any illegal acts of violence or detention, or any act of depredation, committed for private ends by the crew or the passengers of a private ship or a private aircraft, and directed-

(i) on the high seas, against another ship or aircraft, or against persons or property on board such ship or aircraft;

(ii) against a ship, aircraft, persons or property in a place outside the jurisdiction of any State;

(b) any act of voluntary participation in the operation of a ship or of an aircraft with knowledge of facts making it a pirate ship or aircraft;

(c) any act of inciting or of intentionally facilitating an act described in subparagraph (a) or (b).[78]

Article 110 of UNCLOS authorizes warships to visit and/or inspect ships on the high seas that are suspected of engagement in piracy. Although the United States is not party to UNCLOS, the Convention on the High Seas also authorizes the right of visitation/inspection of vessels suspected of being engaged in piracy.[79] States, under both the Convention on the High Seas and UNCLOS, are authorized to seize a pirate ship, or a ship taken by piracy and under the control of the pirates, and arrest the persons and seize the property on board.[80] The courts of the State whose forces carry out a seizure may decide the penalties to be imposed on the pirates.[81]

The SUA Convention further expands on the judicial treatment of pirates. Its main purpose is "to ensure that appropriate action is taken against persons committing unlawful acts against ships."[82]

Unlawful acts include, but are not limited to, the seizure of ships; acts of violence against persons on board ships; and the placing of devices on board a ship which are likely to destroy or damage it.[83] The SUA Convention calls on parties to the agreement to make its enumerated offenses "punishable by appropriate penalties which take into account the grave nature of those offenses."[84] The United States criminalizes acts of piracy[85] and foreigners or U.S. citizens that commit acts of piracy are subject to imprisonment for life.[86] While it appears that U.S. law is sufficient to address the criminality of piracy, this may not be the case in other countries. Additionally, even with comprehensive criminal laws, the logistics related to the enforcement of the laws may be an impediment to their use.

Contact Group on Piracy off the Coast of Somalia (CGPCS)

Based on Resolution 1851, the Bush Administration led the formation of a multilateral Contact Group on Piracy off the Coast of Somalia (CGPCS) made up of 24 member governments and five regional and international organizations.[87] The Contact Group held its first meeting in January 2009 and identified six tasks for itself: 1) improving operational and information support to counter-piracy operations, 2) establishing a counter-piracy coordination mechanism, 3) strengthening judicial frameworks for arrest, prosecution and detention of pirates, 4) strengthening commercial shipping self-awareness and other capabilities, 5) pursuing improved diplomatic and public information efforts, and 6) tracking financial flows related to piracy.[88] In support of these goals, four working groups make recommendations at periodic meetings of the Contact Group secretariat on relevant military/operational, judicial, diplomatic, and public information aspects of regional and international anti-piracy efforts. The goals of these efforts are to improve operational coordination, information sharing, and the effectiveness of legal enforcement activities among all international actors combating piracy in the region.

The membership of the CGPCS has grown to approximately 60 member governments and seven regional organizations. CGPCS meetings in 2010 provided updates on the efforts of working groups and made a number of suggestions and appeals, including calling for further donations to counter-piracy trust funds that support regional capacity building; requesting additional maritime patrol aircraft, oil tankers, helicopter-capable ships and military Vessel Protection Detachments and boarding teams; and identifying the need for more robust global efforts to track and freeze proceeds and support funds associated with piracy.[89] These requests dovetail with the findings of the September 2010 GAO report referenced above, which called on the U.S. government to improve interagency coordination and program monitoring to improve performance in these areas. Some of the international community's efforts to address CGPCS suggestions are discussed in this report. The Contact Group's most recent meeting was held in March 2011 in New York. Earlier that month, the United States convened an ad hoc meeting to develop a strategy and action plan to address the financial aspects of piracy.

Within the Contact Group, U.S. officials have led the efforts of a working group seeking to improve awareness and implementation of self-defence best practices in the shipping and insurance industries. Since May 2009, the United States and several other governments have signed a Commitment to Best Management Practices to Avoid, Deter or Delay Acts of Piracy (the so-called "New York Declaration"), including popular ship registry countries such as Panama, Liberia, the Bahamas, and the Marshall Islands.

The International Maritime Organization (IMO) and the Djibouti Code of Conduct

The International Maritime Organization (IMO)[90] has had an international anti-piracy program since the late 1990s and has successfully engaged on a multilateral basis in other regions to improve anti-piracy cooperation. Cooperative mechanisms for managing the security of the waters off the Horn of Africa are being developed, as called for by the IMO[91] and encouraged by Resolution 1851.[92] The IMO began sponsoring consultation meetings for the region in 2005, which led to the development of a draft cooperative framework agreement in early 2008.

In January 2009, representatives of 17 regional governments met at an IMO-sponsored meeting in Djibouti and adopted a Code of Conduct concerning the Repression of Piracy and Armed Robbery against Ships in the western Indian Ocean and the Gulf of Aden.[93] Most regional governments[94] have signed the Code of Conduct, which remains open for signature by other parties. Three regional facilities—the Maritime Rescue Coordination Centre in Mombasa, Kenya, the Sub-Regional Coordination Centre in Dar es Salaam, Tanzania, and a new regional maritime information center in Sana'a, Yemen—support the information sharing components of the agreement. The parties also agreed to resolutions on technical cooperation and the establishment of a regional training center in Djibouti. In September 2009, Japan made an initial contribution of $14 million to a trust fund dedicated to supporting the IMO's Djibouti Code-related training and capacity building operations. The IMO is assisting Member States to bring their national anti-piracy legislation into line with the Code.

The Djibouti Code of Conduct discussions have led to the creation of mechanisms to promote greater cooperation between the Somali TFG and the regional governments of Somaliland and Puntland. The three parties agreed in January 2010 to form a three-member technical committee, the Somali Contact Group on Counter-Piracy, also known as the "Kampala Process," to coordinate their efforts. During that meeting they agreed on a draft anti-piracy law and began to work on laws related to the transfer of prisoners. They signed a memorandum of understanding to cooperate on counter-piracy issues in April 2010. Both Puntland and Somaliland have interdicted and arrested suspected pirates and accepted them for trial.

A similar cooperative framework developed by the IMO, the littoral states of the Strait of Malacca, and other Asian governments has been in force since 2006. Known as the Regional Cooperation Agreement on Combating Piracy and Armed Robbery against ships in Asia (ReCAAP),[95] the agreement established procedures for coordinating responses to piracy and sharing best practices among law enforcement and security personnel. The ReCAAP Information Sharing Center (ISC) in Singapore now serves as the principal clearinghouse for piracy reporting and response coordination.[96] These steps, taken in conjunction with other regional agreements between Malaysia, Indonesia and Singapore to coordinate anti-piracy patrols in the Straits of Malacca and surrounding waters, have been successful in reducing piracy in that region. The negotiation of the bilateral and multilateral initiatives in the Straits of Malacca region highlighted several issues that may be of interest to parties seeking to establish similar programs in the Horn of Africa region, namely the importance of addressing local concerns over sovereignty, territorial water rights, and the presence of foreign military forces in regional waters.

Preventing and Disrupting Pirate Attacks

Private Sector and Shipping Industry Responses

Private sector and shipping industry responses to the threat of piracy in the waters off the Horn of Africa have varied. In addition to altering financial decisions based on higher insurance costs, some accounts suggest that shipment navigation patterns have changed in response to the threat of piracy, with some vessels preferring to circumnavigate the southern Cape of Good Hope rather than risk attack in the Gulf of Aden. Crews also have developed a number of unique countermeasures and best practices in their attempts to ward off and resist pirate attacks. The use of water cannons, fire hoses, and passive sonic defenses has become more widespread. Initial industry surveys suggested that ships that operate at speeds above 15 knots[97] and that have higher freeboards[98] have proven less susceptible to pirate attack. However, the U.S. Office of Naval Intelligence warned in March 2010 of “pirates' increasing ability to board any vessel regardless of high freeboard.”[99] The use of safe rooms, or “citadels” by crew during attacks has proven a successful mechanism for avoiding capture in several cases. Debates about the use of armed guards continue among shipping industry representatives, government officials, and observers worldwide (see “Options for Improving the Immediate Security of Merchant Ships”).

The IMO and other bodies such as the International Chamber of Commerce International Maritime Bureau (ICC-IMB) have developed detailed guidance and recommendations, commonly known as “Best Management Practices,” for governments and commercial vessels seeking to prevent, deter, and respond to pirate attacks.[100] The IMB manages a 24-hour piracy reporting center in Kuala Lumpur, Malaysia, which seeks to serve as the global, one-stop shop for piracy reporting and piracy threat information distribution for commercial vessels. The IMB also works with other regional information centers to collect and disseminate threat and situation reporting. For the Horn of Africa region, the IMB and European Union Maritime Security Center-Horn of Africa (MSC-HOA) issue periodic “Industry Updates” detailing recent trends in pirate attacks and making recommendations to vessels transiting regional waters.[101]

Combined Task Force 151 and Other Navies' “National Escort Systems”

U.S. Naval Forces Central Command (NAVCENT) commands the Combined Maritime Forces (CMF) operating in the Arabian/Persian Gulf, Gulf of Oman, Gulf of Aden, Red Sea, Arabian Sea, and Indian Ocean. In January 2009, the command established Combined Task Force 151 (CTF-151), with the sole mission of conducting anti-piracy operations in the Gulf of Aden and the waters off the Somali coast in the Indian Ocean. That role had previously been filled by CTF-150, which continues to perform counterterrorism and other maritime security operations as it has since 2001.

In August 2008, CTF 150 and partner forces agreed to the establishment of a Maritime Security Patrol Area (MSPA) in the Gulf of Aden to serve as a dedicated, more secure transit zone for merchant vessels. The MSPA has been credited, in part, with lowering the success rate of Somali pirates in the Gulf of Aden transit zone. Within the MSPA, eastbound and westbound Internationally Recommended Transit Corridors (IRTC) have been established "to de-conflict commercial transit traffic with Yemeni fishermen, provide a measure of traffic separation, and allow maritime forces to conduct deterrent operations in the [Gulf of Aden] with a greater degree of flexibility."[102] All U.S.-flagged vessels transiting the Gulf of Aden have been directed to plan their voyages using the IRTC.

The list of countries participating in CTF-151 is fluid and consists of personnel and approximately two dozen ships from 25 countries, including the United States, the United Kingdom, Canada, Denmark, France, Germany, Greece, Italy, the Netherlands, Pakistan, Saudi Arabia, Spain, South Korea, Turkey and Yemen. CTF-151 is currently under the command of the Singapore Navy, and has previously been commanded by the U.S. Navy, the Korean Navy, and the Turkish Navy. The Task force's daily operations are managed onboard the *TCG Gokceada*, while the operations of the Combined Maritime Forces, which contributes to CTF-151, are coordinated from the NAVCENT command center in Bahrain. U.S. Coast Guard Law Enforcement Detachments (LEDETs) operate aboard CTF-151 vessels and perform support and advisory missions during boarding operations and provide training to task force personnel on evidence procedures, maritime law, and related issues.

Other countries, most notably Russia, China, and India, have deployed naval forces to the region to participate in monitoring and anti-piracy "national escort system" operations. From an operational perspective, while these countries have not formally and fully coordinated their policies with CTF-151, there are ongoing communication efforts. A military coordination mechanism known as Shared Awareness and De-confliction (SHADE) coordinates the activities of coalition forces and Russia, China, India, and Japan through monthly meetings.

In January 2010, China agreed to assign one of its naval vessels to patrol the IRTC in coordination with CTF-151 and other coalition forces, and signaled that it may seek a rotating co-chairmanship role in future SHADE gatherings. Naval observers and officials in the United States have noted the engagement of China with particular interest, as Chinese naval operations in the Horn of Africa region demonstrate the Chinese government's desire and ability to protect international shipping lanes far from China's shores. China's recent offer to assist European Union naval forces with World Food Program escort operations indicate China's willingness to expand its responsibilities in the region, which may require an expansion of its naval deployment. In June 2010, 19 Chinese sailors were captured by Somali pirates aboard the *MV Golden Blessing*: their shipping company paid a $3 million dollar ransom to secure their release in November 2010. Days later, 29 Chinese sailors were kidnapped by Somali pirates in the Arabian Sea aboard the vessel Yuan Xiang.[103]

NATO: Operation Ocean Shield

In October 2008, the North Atlantic Treaty Organization (NATO) deployed the first of two Standing NATO Maritime Groups to conduct anti-piracy operations in the Horn of Africa region. The first deployment, named Operation Allied Provider, served as a temporary protection force for World Food Program assistance shipments in the region. In December 2008, NATO ended Operation Allied Provider and transitioned WFP protection responsibilities to the European Union's new naval operation (see "European Union: Operation ATALANTA" below).

In March 2009, NATO launched a new anti-piracy mission, Operation Allied Protector, under the command of Standing NATO Maritime Group 1 (SNMG1). According to NATO, the forces participating in Operation Allied Protector acted to "deter, defend against and disrupt pirate activities." The Maritime Group was originally scheduled to perform temporary anti-piracy missions as it transited the Horn region en route to South East Asia and as it returned in June 2009. In April 2009, NATO officials cancelled planned SNMG1 visits to Singapore and Australia and extended the Operation Allied Protector mission until June 20, 2009.

In August 2009, NATO replaced Operation Allied Protector with a new anti-piracy mission, Operation Ocean Shield, under the command of Standing NATO Maritime Group 2 (SNMG2). In March 2010, NATO extended the operation through the end of 2012. Like its predecessor missions, Operation Ocean Shield has a primary responsibility to deter and respond to piracy, while participating in capacity building efforts with regional governments. In relation to the latter aspect of the mission, the Group flagship has hosted maritime officials from the Puntland regional government and visited the Somali port of Bossaso in the northern province of Bari (see Figure 2, "Map of Somalia") for consultations with officials responsible for port security and maritime transportation.[104] On January 11, 2011, the Dutch commander of Operation Ocean Shield was hosted by his Chinese counterpart at sea for consultations in an unplanned rendezvous. The following ships were participating in Operation Ocean Shield in April 2011: *HNLMS Tromp* (Flagship)—Netherlands, *USS Bainbridge*—United States, *HDMS Esbern Snare*—Denmark, *USS Stephen W Groves* —United States of America, and *TCG Giresun*—Turkey.

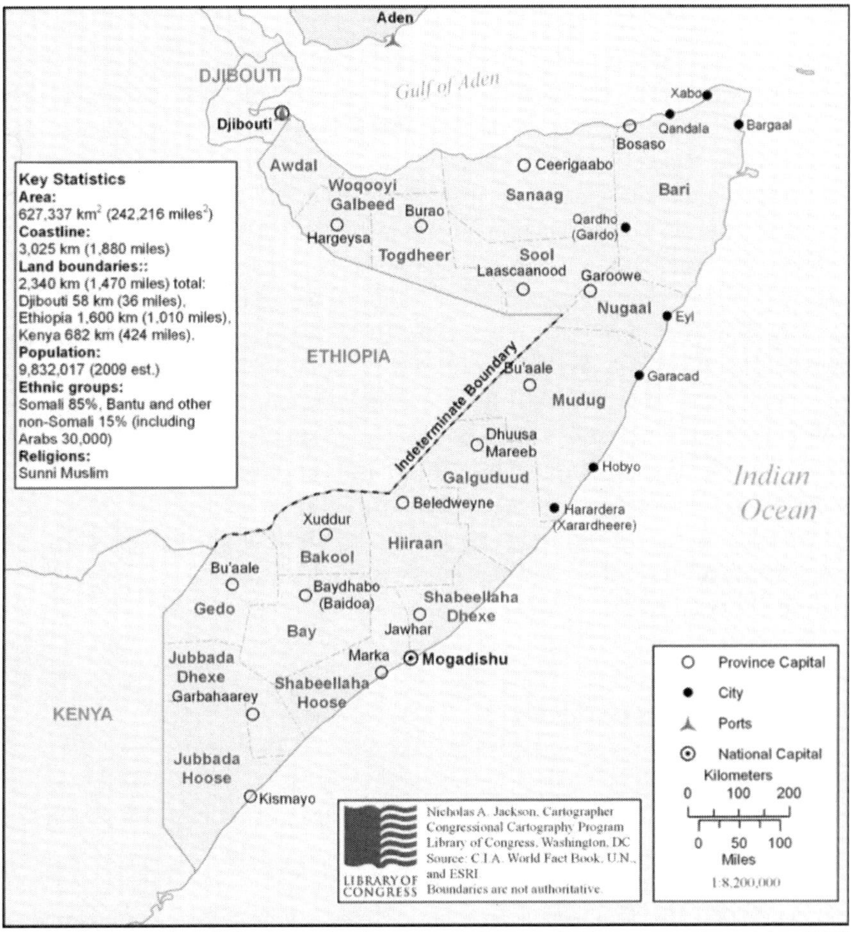

Source: Congressional Cartography Program, Library of Congress, adapted by CRS Graphics. Statistics from Central Intelligence Agency, *The World Factbook*.

Figure 2. Somalia Map.

European Union: Operation ATALANTA

In December 2008, the European Union launched EU NAVFOR Operation ATALANTA, its first naval operation under the framework of the European Security and Defense Policy (ESDP). Forces participating in Operation ATALANTA have been tasked with providing protection for WFP vessels and merchant vessels and are authorized to "employ the necessary measures, including the use of force, to deter, prevent and intervene in order to bring an end to acts of piracy and armed robbery which may be committed in the areas where they are present."[105] EUNAVFOR also promised protection for AMISOM supply ships. In December 2010, the European Council extended the mandate for Operation ATALANTA through December 2012. According to the European Union, the operation will involve up to twenty ships and over 1,800 personnel over its full term. To date, Belgium, France, Germany, Greece, Italy, Luxemburg, the Netherlands, Spain, and Sweden have made permanent contributions of forces and personnel to the operation, as has Norway (which is not a member of the EU), and other EU member states support the operation's headquarters. Finland contributed its first warship to the effort in February 2011. In coordination with the deployment, EU NAVFOR also has established an online center known as Maritime Security Center-Horn of Africa (MSC-HOA) for transiting ships to record their ships' movements voluntarily and to receive updated threat information.[106] Similar voluntary tracking and reporting services are provided by the United Kingdom Maritime Trade Operations office in Dubai and the U.S. Navy's Maritime Liaison Office in Bahrain.

Prosecuting Acts of Piracy

An estimated 17 countries around the world have prosecuted over 800 pirates in their courts, including, in the region most affected by Somali piracy, Kenya, the Seychelles, Yemen, the Maldives, and India. Many observers report, however, that prosecutions do not appear to be having a deterrent effect on young Somalis joining pirate gangs. Some suggest that many Somalis believe they will not be punished for their crimes, given that local authorities, with some exceptions, lack the capacity to detain and prosecute suspects. Experts also point to a so-called "catch and release" practice by many international naval forces, in which, by some estimates, 90% of pirates captured by patrols are released because no jurisdiction is prepared to prosecute them.[107] Recent reports suggest that only 93 out of 770 pirates detained by EUNAVFOR, for example, have been sent to court since December 2008.[108]

In January 2010, the CGPCS approved the final terms for an anti-piracy trust fund, which is being administered by the United Nations Office of Drugs and Crime (UNODC). As of late 2010, the trust fund had received $3.66 million in donations, and had approved seven projects worth $2.41 million for prosecution and detention improvements in the Seychelles, Kenya, and Somalia. According to U.S. officials, Kenya, which has taken responsibility for prosecuting the most pirate suspects to date, has indicated that there are limits to their ability to continue to accept pirate suspects captured by international navies for trial.[109] In 2010, the Seychelles signed agreements to prosecute pirates detained at sea and in December 2010 sentenced nine pirates to 22 years each. The capacity of prisons in Kenya and the Seychelles remains limited; facilities in Kenya have benefited from trust fund-supported improvements.

The February 2011 report by the U.N. Secretary-General's Special Advisor on Legal Issues Related to Piracy off the Coast of Somalia, Jack Lang, provides a broad range of options for the international community to consider on the issue of prosecution. It contains 25 proposals to assist countries, particularly those in the region, to prosecute and imprison pirates, and encourages all countries to incorporate the crime of piracy in their domestic laws and to establish universal jurisdiction for acts of piracy. Several countries are currently doing so, including France, Japan, and Tanzania. The report also calls for governments to adapt their legal framework for detention at sea to address human rights and operational constraints currently facing counter-piracy patrols.

Lang's report furthermore explores the ongoing debate on whether to create an international criminal tribunal or to further strengthen regional capacities, including those of Somali authorities. Lang's report proposes direct support from the international community for prosecutions (and incarcerations) by Somaliland and Puntland. The report suggests that specialized piracy courts be created in Somaliland and Puntland, and that, given security concerns, a Somali extraterritorial court be established in Arusha, Africa's "legal capital," to address prosecutions that cannot be currently handled in Mogadishu. Under the proposal, each court would have universal jurisdiction, with the exception of Somaliland, which will only prosecute its citizens or those in its territorial waters. Lang suggest that UNODC could have the Puntland and extraterritorial court operational 8 months, given ongoing UNODC efforts to rehabilitate Puntland's correctional capacity. UNODC has recently completed efforts to rehabilitate a prison and train correctional staff in the Somaliland capital of Hargeisa. These efforts are critical to addressing concerns by many governments currently conducting counterpiracy patrols, given that prison conditions are considered, according to the U.N. Secretary-General, "harsh and life threatening."[110]

United Nations Office on Drugs and Crime (UNODC): "Shipriders" and Capacity Building

Under the auspices of Resolution 1851 and in conjunction with the judicial working group of the CGPCS, the United Nations Office on Drugs and Crime is implementing a project to facilitate regional law enforcement participation in anti-piracy enforcement efforts off the coast of Somalia.[111] The program focuses on providing judicial capacity building assistance to regional states and facilitating so-called "shiprider" arrangements in which regional law enforcement personnel are seconded to international vessels to perform anti-piracy arrest and investigation functions. The United States has shiprider agreements with a number of Western Hemisphere governments to facilitate maritime security operations in waters of shared concern.

In general, shiprider arrangements are designed to address the logistical and legal challenges inherent in multilateral naval enforcement efforts in remote areas or where the capacity of regional governments does not allow for the provision of sufficient security. With regard to current operations in the Horn of Africa region, long transport times, limited military resources, legal limitations on the operations of military personnel, and complex differences in jurisdictional standards and requirements would complicate the arrest and prosecution by the varied non-regional forces operating under Resolution 1851.

In order to help regional governments meet the added resource requirements that the arrest, detention, and prosecution of Somali pirate suspects would create, the UNODC is also providing judicial capacity building assistance, in coordination with the European Commission and other donors, including the United States. The UNODC has been designated the chair for the donor trust fund authorized by the CGPCS.

Issues for Congress and Policy Options

Attacks by Somali pirates on U.S. flagged vessels or U.S.-bound commerce to date have been high-profile but limited in number, however the broader threat that Somali piracy poses to free navigation in the Gulf of Aden and the west Indian Ocean has global implications. The U.S. government has identified piracy in the waters off Somalia as a direct threat to national security interests, as have several foreign governments, notably China, Russia, and the EU member states. Policies developed by the Bush Administration to address the threat have been revisited and enhanced by the Obama Administration, and recent statements by senior U.S. officials suggest that these policies remain under review. Congress appropriates funding and provides oversight for a number of Administration efforts with implications for piracy in the region.

The risk of attack in the waters off Somalia is unlikely to disappear in the near term. Most defense analysts acknowledge that while the unprecedented level of naval patrols in the area— conducted by more than twenty nations— has deterred some attacks, the area is simply too vast to prevent all incidents. When the *Maersk Alabama* was attacked in 2009, the closest naval vessel, the *U.S.S. Bainbridge,* was approximately 300 nautical miles away. Similarly, the *U.S.S. Bainbridge* was only able to arrive on the scene of the aborted attack on the *Liberty Sun* a reported six hours after the attack ended. The continuing anti-piracy operations of international navies also comes at significant cost, as governments around the world weigh budget priorities and military requirements in other theaters of operation. Secretary of State Hillary Clinton told Congress in March 2011, "we have put together an international coalition, but, frankly, we're just not, in my view, getting enough out of it," noting that international counter-piracy patrols do not appear to be having a deterrent effect and that they payment of ransoms continues to exacerbate the problem.[112] She has tasked the State Department, in collaboration with the Department of Defense, with developing a more comprehensive approach.

Like terrorism, acts of piracy in African waters pose a transnational security threat that emanates from areas plagued by conflict, weak governance, and economic insecurity. Continuing conflict in Somalia and Yemen illustrate the unstable regional context surrounding current counter-piracy operations. Regional security forces have limited maritime capability, and many governments have prioritized the development of their armies at the expense of navies or coast guards. That has changed to some extent in recent years, as international studies have highlighted the threat to local economies posed by illegal fishing, in addition to more traditional maritime security threats. Regional coordination and intelligence sharing also is weak.

The United States and its international partners have used various policy tools to address similarly complex security circumstances in other regions. However, ongoing U.S. and international security operations in environments such as Afghanistan, Pakistan, Iraq, and Colombia suggest that military intervention and foreign assistance require political consensus, political will, local partnership, and significant coordination in order to be successful. Maritime security efforts in the Persian Gulf, the Caribbean, the waters of West Africa, and the Strait of Malacca have had the same requirements. While short term results in containing other transnational threats have proven to be achievable, the long-term ability of international intervention to eliminate these threats is less certain in the absence of committed and capable regional and local actors.

Secretary Clinton stated in her remarks to Congress in March 2011, "its hard to imagine that we're going to be able to resolve this until we go after their land-based ports."[113] Both civilian and military officials have repeatedly stated, however, that the problem of Somali piracy will not ultimately be solved militarily. The Secretary of the Navy testified in March 2011,

> We are treating the symptoms of piracy, rather than its fundamental cause: Somalia`s failure as a state. Despite the international community`s commitment, piracy has both continued to increase and move further offshore, a measure of pirate resiliency and the strong economic incentives that underpin it. Nine of ten pirates captured are ultimately freed as there is often insufficient evidence or political will to prosecute them, or to incarcerate them after conviction. We strongly endorse additional international efforts to address these concerns.[114]

The effective use of force against pirate strongholds in coastal towns would likely require significant military planning and considerable resources in order to avoid or minimize civilian casualties. The number of naval ships that would be needed to completely halt piracy in the Gulf of Aden and the waters of Somalia's eastern coast is probably much larger than the force currently operating there. By some estimates, as many as 60 ships might be required to fully suppress piracy in the Gulf of Aden alone. The adjoining area of concern in the Indian Ocean off Somalia's eastern coast, which has been measured at more than two million square miles, is much larger, so completely halting piracy in that area would likely require an even larger number of ships.

Congressional Action

The 111th Congress explored options for protecting maritime traffic in the Horn of Africa region and around the world. H.R. 3376, the U.S. Mariner and

Vessel Protection Act of 2009, aimed to eliminate liability for death or injury caused by the use of force during the self-defense of U.S. mariners against acts of piracy (see "Arming Merchant Ships" below). S. 3639, the Maritime Transportation Security Act of 2010, introduced in July 2010, would have eliminated liability for monetary damages in some cases of self-defense against piracy at sea. The bill also would have directed the department overseeing the Coast Guard to work through the IMO to promote coordinated anti-piracy action and to ensure similar limitations on liability. The monetary liability provisions of the Senate bill were incorporated into Section 912 of the Coast Guard Authorization Act of 2010 (H.R. 3619, P.L. 111-281) enacted October 15, 2010.

Section 3505 of the FY2010 National Defense Authorization Act (NDAA, H.R. 2647, P.L. 111- 84) requires any vessel carrying cargo for the Department of Defense in areas of high risk of piracy to be equipped with "appropriate non-lethal defense measures to protect the vessel, crew, and cargo from unauthorized seizure at sea." Section 3506 of the Act further required the Administration to report on steps taken by the U.S. government to facilitate the embarkation of armed security teams aboard U.S.-flagged vessels carrying U.S. government cargo in high risk areas.[115] The House version of H.R. 2647 would have required the Secretary of Defense to embark military personnel on board U.S.-flagged vessels carrying cargos owned by the U.S. government if a vessel is traveling in a high risk area and is determined by the Coast Guard to be at risk of being boarded by pirates. The Senate version of the bill did not include these measures.

Congress has stressed that the U.S. government and others must address the piracy problem both at sea and on land. H.Rept. 111-166, accompanying H.R. 2647, expressed concern with continuing safe havens for Somali pirates, noting that "there does not appear to be a strategy for dealing with the organizations ashore in Somalia." S.Rept. 111-35, accompanying the FY2010 NDAA, stressed the need for a "holistic approach," emphasizing the need for the commercial shipping industry to develop effective piracy countermeasures to protect its ships and crews.

Two resolutions passed by the House and Senate in April 2009 commended the crew of the *Maersk Alabama*, Captain Richard Phillips, and the U.S. military for its efforts in rescuing Captain Phillips and serving in anti-piracy missions (H.Res. 339 and S.Res. 108). The Senate resolution called on President Obama to "work with the international community and the transitional government of Somalia to develop a comprehensive strategy to address both the burgeoning problem of piracy and its root causes."

As the 112th Congress has commenced its deliberations, Somali pirate attacks continue at an increased rate, and the capture of the *Quest* and killing of four Americans in early 2011 have contributed to a renewed debate on U.S. efforts to address the threat. In March 2011, the House Transportation and Infrastructure Subcommittee on Coast Guard and Maritime Transportation held a hearing on the U.S. Response to maritime piracy. Among the issues raised by Members for further exploration was that of tracking ransom payments in a manner similar to tracking terrorist financing. According to the September 2010 study conducted by the GAO, "officials at Justice, State, and Defense agree that information their agencies gather on pirate finances is not being systematically analyzed, and it is unclear if any agency is using it to identify and apprehend pirate leaders or financiers."[116] The 112th Congress has not, to date, introduced legislation related to the issue of maritime piracy or the specific threat posed in the waters off Somalia.

Oversight of U.S. Military Forces and U.S. Foreign Assistance

U.S. military engagement in the region is divided among two geographic combatant Commands. U.S. Central Command's area of responsibility (AOR) includes the waters of the Gulf of Aden and those off the eastern Somali coast, while the AOR of U.S. Africa Command (AFRICOM), which became fully operational in 2008, encompasses the African continent.[117] To date, much of the U.S. military's anti-piracy response has been conducted at sea, by Central Command (CENTCOM). On land, AFRICOM provides security assistance to several regional maritime security forces, few of which have "blue water capacity" (the ability to operate far from shore). CENTCOM provides similar assistance to the Yemeni coast guard.

Oversight of U.S. Navy anti-piracy operations focuses on forces associated with CTF-151 and with NATO's Operation Ocean Shield. Several U.S.-homeported Navy ships support the deployment of U.S. Navy ships operating on a continuous basis in the areas where Somali pirates are active. As such, the commitment of a single additional U.S. Navy ship to the area can affect the Navy's ability to perform missions in other parts of the world.

U.S. military operations in the region are not limited to anti-piracy efforts. The United States has conducted anti-terrorism activities in the Horn of Africa and in Yemen for over a decade, including the naval Combined Task Forces established as part of Operation Enduring Freedom. Djibouti has hosted the U.S.-led Combined Joint Task Force–Horn of Africa (CJTF-HOA) at a semipermanent Forward Operating Site, known as Camp Lemonnier, since 2003, with approximately 2,000 U.S. military personnel in residence. The command authority for CJTFHOA, formerly under CENTCOM, has been transferred to AFRICOM. Its efforts initially focused primarily on countering violent extremism in the region, but the Task Force's activities have expanded in recent years to include a wide variety of activities aimed at building the capacity of regional militaries to respond to more general threats, such as natural disasters and armed conflict. CJTF-HOA personnel provide training to the region's security forces on counterterrorism, maritime security, disaster response, and peacekeeping.

As mentioned above, the United States conducts a variety of maritime security assistance programs in East Africa and Yemen. In Kenya, for example, the United States provides maritime security assistance to both the Kenyan Navy and an array of agencies, including the Kenya Wildlife Service, revenue authority, and police, to address a range of threats, from smuggling and illegal fishing to terrorism. The U.S. also began support for a regional Maritime Center of Excellence in Mombasa in 2009; courses at the Center are attended by participants from throughout East Africa. Several African countries, including Djibouti, Kenya, Tanzania, and Yemen, have received U.S. support for the installation of radar systems that provide enhanced maritime domain awareness.

Congress expanded the Department of Defense's Section 1206 "train and equip" authority in FY2009 to include assistance for civilian maritime security forces to conduct counterterrorism operations. Counter-piracy is not mentioned. However, several FY2009 Section 1206 programs support increased maritime capacity to address terrorist threats in the waters affected by Somali piracy, including programs for Djibouti, Yemen, Mozambique, Mauritius, Tanzania, and the Seychelles. In August 2009, AFRICOM and the government of the Seychelles announced an agreement governing Operation Ocean Look, which allows the U.S. military to operate P-3 Orion aircraft and unmanned aerial vehicles from the Seychelles in an effort to improve maritime surveillance in regional waters.[118]

U.N. Security Council Resolution 1851 "calls on Member States to assist the TFG, at its request and with notification to the Secretary-General, to strengthen its operational capacity to bring to justice those who are using Somali territory to plan, facilitate or undertake criminal acts of piracy and armed robbery at sea."

The Obama Administration may seek to expand current assistance programs for regional and Somali actors subject to congressional appropriations and authorization and in accordance with U.N. Security Council resolutions. As noted above, the Obama Administration has obligated Peacekeeping Operations (PKO) funding to provide equipment, logistical support, and basing facilities for the African Union Mission to Somalia and to support Somali security sector reform. While these funds have largely been directed toward improving Somali capacity to counter threats from insurgents and terrorists, to the extent that assistance may improve the overall ability of government forces to operate effectively and assert security control, it could have positive implications for anti-piracy operations in the future. The Administration is requesting $51 million in FY2012 PKO funding to continue these programs.

Although some press reports in 2009 quoted unnamed U.S. officials as stating that the U.S. military may consider launching military attacks against pirate strongholds, U.S. defense officials testified before Congress at that time that although the United States has supported the inclusion in Security Council Resolution 1851 of authorization for anti-piracy operations on land, there were no U.S. military plans to do so.[119]

Various parts of the U.S. government continue to encourage Somali figures in the Transitional Federal Government and in the region of Puntland to take action against pirate safe havens ashore. Overall, the Administration has not signaled any major policy changes from the National Security Council *Partnership and Action Plan*, which states that the United States "will work with concerned governments and international organizations to disrupt and dismantle pirate bases to the fullest extent permitted by national law."

The Use of Private Companies to Train Somali Maritime Forces

In addition to security assistance received from foreign donors, the Somali Transitional Federal Government (TFG) and the semi-autonomous Somali regions of Puntland and Somaliland have employed the services of private companies to train and support their security forces, and, on occasion, to help enforce security in their territories and surrounding waters.

Such companies have been operating in Somalia for decades, providing an array of services, from convoy security for humanitarian aid deliveries to security escorts and personal security details for high-ranking individuals.

Private industry also employs the services of these companies. In 1999, for example, the government of Puntland, which accounts for roughly one-third of Somalia's coastline, hired a British firm to train a maritime security force to counter illegal fishing. According to some reports, illegal fishing and pirate attacks dropped in Puntland's waters during the contract period, through 2001.[120] Puntland subsequently employed the services of several local contractors, according to reports, with less success.[121] Neighboring Somaliland secured the services of a Norwegian firm in 2006 to improve security standards at the port of Berbera and to train harbor security forces and local police. The firm's forces have reportedly apprehended pirates and brought them before the region's courts.[122]

The TFG has also looked to hire private companies to train its maritime security service. In 2005, the TFG reportedly awarded a U.S. firm with a $50 million contract to create a coast guard to counter piracy. The U.S. State Department's Bureau of Arms Control subsequently determined that the contract would breach the U.N. arms embargo on Somalia and issued a cease and desist order.[123] Some private security companies have drawn considerable criticism in recent years for their actions in Iraq and Afghanistan, prompting questions related to accountability and broader government regulation of the industry. Reported contracts between an African firm, Saracen International, and both the government of Puntland and the TFG to train security forces recently raised questions in the media. The Puntland government acknowledged its relationship with Saracen, stating that the company had been contracted to train and mentor a new law enforcement entity, the Puntland Marine Force, to counter piracy and illegal fishing.[124] Somalia's Transitional Federal Parliament complained about the lack of transparency in TFG contracting and, after a series of controversial media reports in late 2010 regarding private security companies in Somalia, the parliament demanded that the TFG suspend the operations of several companies, including Saracen.[125] The Puntland government reportedly suspended its contact with Saracen in March 2011. The suspended contracts or any future such arrangements would require notification to the U.N. Monitoring Group on Somalia, per U.N. resolutions.

Challenges in Prosecuting Pirates

Questions regarding legal jurisdiction, due process for detained pirate suspects, and the role of foreign military forces in anti-piracy law enforcement activities complicate current U.S. and international operations against pirates in the Horn of Africa region. The most immediate legal concern associated with anti-piracy operations are jurisdictional questions that arise based on the location of pirate attacks and/or international naval interventions, the nationalities of crew members, and the countries of registry and/or ownership of any seized vessels.[126] Multiple governments may be able to assert legal jurisdiction, depending on the specifics of the incident, but the exercise of universal jurisdiction established under UNCLOS for acts of piracy is optional. Political will may be present in some countries, but many governments lack sufficient laws and judicial capacity to effectively prosecute suspected pirates. The disposition of property and insurance claims for vessels involved in piracy also raises complex legal questions. A developing legal issue concerns the prosecution of juveniles participating in acts of piracy. Reports suggest that some of the Somali pirates are teenage minors,[127] and therefore could have a defense of infancy in certain jurisdictions that may assert jurisdiction over the offense.[128]

To date, some of these legal and law enforcement challenges have been addressed through the establishment of bilateral agreements by the United States, the United Kingdom, the European Union and others with governments in the Horn of Africa region, particularly with Kenya, which was the first country in the region to exercise universal jurisdiction, in 2006. Some agreements concluded to date define procedures for the detention, transfer, and prosecution of captured pirate suspects. For example, suspected pirates captured by U.S. military forces may be transferred to Kenyan custody for prosecution according to the terms of a bilateral memorandum of understanding signed in January 2009. The EU reached a similar agreement with Kenya in March 2009. In 2009 and 2010, Kenyan courts sentenced 50 Somalis captured by international navies to prison for piracy crimes. In March 2010, however, Kenyan officials announced that they were suspending the acceptance of new pirate suspects for prosecution, pending further negotiation with the United States and other coalition parties. In November 2010, Kenya's second highest court ruled that it did not have the jurisdiction to try pirates captured outside Kenya's territorial waters; the country's Attorney General has appealed the decision.[129] According to the UNODC, Kenya was holding over 120 piracy suspects in early 2011. The Seychelles has also reached agreements to accept the transfer of pirate suspects for prosecution, and Tanzania has amended its laws to allow the prosecution of pirates captured outside its territorial waters.

The U.S. Department of Justice (DOJ) has conducted several piracy workshops for foreign prosecutors, police, and maritime security personnel. For example, the United States has provided capacity building assistance to Kenya's Department of Public Prosecutions since 2005, and a resident legal advisor from DOJ provides the Kenyan government with assistance in piracy cases. Other international donors have become increasingly engaged, and UNODC is currently implementing a substantial capacity building program funded by the European Commission, as noted above. Efforts also are underway to establish mechanisms for regional law enforcement personnel to serve as shipriders on coalition vessels and to expand the anti-piracy law enforcement and judicial capacities of neighboring states.

Ultimately, however, one of the greatest challenges to prosecuting Somali pirates appears to be determining where to incarcerate them. Hundreds of suspected pirates have been apprehended by international navies in recent years. Many countries in the region lack the prison capacity to take on the additional burden. Additionally, some European countries have been unwilling to transfer suspected pirates for prosecution to countries in the region whose detention facilities may not meet international human rights standards. The United Nations and the international Contact Group are currently exploring new mechanisms to expand the options for incarceration, both in Somalia and the broader region. UNODC efforts to expand and improve corrections facilities in Puntland and Somaliland may contribute to these discussions.

Options for Improving the Immediate Security of Merchant Ships

Risk Reduction and Best Practices

The U.S. Department of Transportation Maritime Administration (MARAD) issues detailed guidance to U.S. mariners transiting the waters off the Horn of Africa region to help ensure their safety and security.[130] Current guidance includes instructions for U.S.-flagged vessels seeking escort support from the U.S. Navy and Combined Maritime Forces participating in coalition naval security operations in the region. As noted above, international bodies such as the International Maritime Organization and the International Maritime Bureau also have revised their recommendations for actions that merchant ships and their crews can take to reduce their risk of being attacked and captured.

These include measures that can be taken before and during pirate attacks. For example, rerouting ships, if possible, allows ships to avoid waters where Somali pirates are known to operate. This option can lengthen operating routes and increase shipping costs, but perhaps not as much as paying an occasional ransom. In transit, effective watch procedures are recommended, since early detection of impending attacks increases the likelihood that avoidance and suppression measures will succeed. Higher ship operating speeds and evasive maneuvers have proven effective in many cases, as have denial systems such as barbed and razor wire and specialized electrical fences for ships. Crew preparation, training, and responses also are credited with reducing risks of successful pirate attacks.

Arming Merchant Ships[131]

Arming merchant ships can be done by either giving arms to the ship's crew, or by hiring armed security teams to ride on the ships. Some observers and industry representatives have advocated for these options as a means of ensuring that there is an immediate security presence aboard vessels to serve as a deterrent or to respond to pirate attacks. Supporters argue that the large geographic distances and limited responsiveness of international naval assets to piracy attacks makes the provision of on-ship security necessary. Others contend that the training of crew members to safely handle weapons does not pose an undue financial or practical burden to shipping companies. However, some merchant ship owners and operators are strongly averse to arming merchant ships, for practical and financial reasons.

U.S. government officials traditionally have expressed concern that merchant ships with armed crew members could pose security or terrorism risks visiting U.S. ports. As noted above, private or military gun battles with pirates can raise the overall level of violence associated with piracy off Somalia, which may increase risks to all merchant mariners on ships operating in that area. Since merchant ship crews are often not trained in the use of weapons, they might not be able to use them very effectively in fighting pirates. If ship crews try to defend themselves with firearms and fail, the pirates might be more likely to kill some of the crew members.

Even if used properly, lighter firearms might not be effective in countering pirates armed with heavier weapons, such as rocket-propelled grenades. Pirates with access to large amounts of money from prior ransom payments can acquire heavier weapons, so as to out-gun the merchant ships. In all cases, fire is a major safety concern, particularly on tanker ships, and gunfire could ignite vapors from the ship's cargo, or the cargo itself.

Financial concerns may discourage the arming of merchant ships. Some industry experts suggest that hiring armed security teams may be more expensive than taking the risk and paying the occasional ransom. Liability for fatal shootings aboard a ship could lead to expensive lawsuits. Since many ports restrict vessels from having weapons on board, commercial ships that make calls at multiple ports along their operating routes could find it difficult to operate along certain routes. Reports suggest that private companies providing armed guards and shipping companies using armed security teams are grappling with these and other related issues in an effort to avoid legal trouble. Hugh Martin, general manager of security firm Hart Security UK has stated that "the amount of effort we put in to ensure we are legal is colossal."[132]

In 2009, the IMO Maritime Safety Committee released the following guidance:

> [F]lag States should strongly discourage the carrying and use of firearms by seafarers for personal protection or for the protection of a ship...the use of unarmed security personnel is a matter for individual shipowners, companies, and ship operators to decide. The carriage of armed security personnel, or the use of military or law-enforcement officers (duly authorized by the Government of the flag State to carry firearms for the security of the ship), should be subject to flag State legislation and policies and is a matter for the flag State to authorize, in consultation with ship owners, companies and ship operators.[133]

Sec. 3506 of the National Defense Authorization Act for FY2010 (H.R. 2647, P.L. 111-84, October 28, 2009) required the Administration to report on its efforts to facilitate the embarkation of armed private security teams on U.S. flagged commercial vessels operating in high risk areas. Items to be reported on include the elimination of restrictions under any regulation or provision of law on the use of armed security teams in high risk areas, the negotiation of bilateral agreements with relevant coastal states, and the development of common training and qualification standards for armed security teams. The report was delivered to Congress in February 2010 and describes numerous advisories the Administration has issued that offer guidance to U.S. flagged commercial vessels. The report also provides detail on U.S. efforts to coordinate with and obtain information from relevant foreign port authorities on the issue of armed security teams.[134]

International Traffic in Arms Regulations (ITAR)

The International Traffic in Arms Regulations (ITAR) may be an area of concern for ship owners desiring to arm their vessels in self-defense against acts of piracy. Section 38 of the Arms Export Control Act (ACEA)[135] authorizes the President to control the export and import of defense articles and defense services. The President, through Executive Order 11958, as amended, delegated the statutory authority to promulgate regulations with respect to exports of defense articles and defense services to the Secretary of State. The resulting regulations are known as the International Traffic in Arms Regulations.[136]

ITAR requires U.S. persons[137] to obtain a license in order to export or import items identified on the United States Munitions List.[138] As defined by regulation, the term "export" includes "sending or taking a defense article out of the United States[139] in any manner."[140] Objects covered by the term "defense article" are found on the United States Munitions List[141] and are classified into 21 separate categories. Categories I and III appear to be most relevant in a discussion regarding protection from acts of piracy because they include firearms (category I) and ammunition (category III) that could be used in the defense of a vessel. Based on the definitions of export and defense articles, a ship owner would be required to obtain a license for the temporary export of firearms and ammunition, or other covered armaments, for use in the defense of a vessel.

There is an exception to the licensing requirement under ITAR for the temporary export of not more than three non-automatic firearms and not more than 1,000 cartridges. To comply with this exception a U.S. person: (1) must declare the temporary export of the firearms and submit to an inspection by a customs officer; (2) must retain the firearms with the person (i.e., not mail the firearms to the destination); and (3) maintain the firearms for that person's exclusive use and not for reexport or transfer of ownership.[142] The regulation makes a distinction between U.S. persons and crew members of vessels, but how the distinction would affect the status of the vessel as an entity is unclear.[143] This exception may be an option available to owners as a way to arm their vessels, without obtaining an export license since the term "U.S. person" is defined to include a corporation, business association, and partnerships, as well as other entities. Additionally, it would appear that individual crew members would be able to temporarily export firearms under the exception. However, crew members using privately owned weapons to defend corporate property could raise significant legal liability issues for both the individuals and the corporation.

The ITAR licensing requirement exception does not supersede prohibitions against exports to certain countries, including, but not limited to countries identified by the United Nations Security Council through a United Nations Arms Embargo.[144] Additionally, a license to export defense articles, or in the alternative obtaining an exemption from the licensing requirement, does not address or satisfy requirements of foreign countries that may exist with respect to operating a vessel in their territorial waters while carrying weapons. The vessel's owner is responsible for knowing and respecting the laws of the foreign country.

Convoys

Some observers argue that U.S. and international naval vessels should provide convoy protection services to ships transiting the Horn of Africa region, particularly the Gulf of Aden. Supporters argue that the direct participation of coalition or other naval assets in merchant ship convoys would eliminate the risks posed by unescorted travel through the Gulf of Aden or areas along the eastern coast of Somalia by cutting down the response times to attempted attacks. However, merchant ship operators may be reluctant to use a convoy system because it can require merchant ships to wait in a certain location for the next scheduled convoy to begin. The delays associated with this waiting can impose costs on ship operators that could be greater than the cost of paying an occasional ransom. The establishment and maintenance of a convoy system over the long term, in the absence of broader efforts to address the root causes of the piracy problem, could pose unacceptable costs for international navies.

Escorts by Navy Ships

As of March 2010, the current MARAD advisory indicates that U.S.-flagged vessels may contact U.S military headquarters in Bahrain to request escort services. Navy or Coast Guard vessels could escort U.S.-flagged commercial ships traveling in the Gulf of Aden, just as U.S. Navy vessels escorted U.S.-flagged ships (including reflagged Kuwaiti oil tankers) in the Persian Gulf in 1987-1988 (aka Operation Earnest Will) so as to protect them from potential Iranian attack during the Iran-Iraq war.

If Navy ships that are forward deployed to the Indian Ocean/Persian Gulf region were diverted from their current missions in that region to a mission of escorting U.S.-flagged commercial ships in the Gulf of Aden, the incremental financial cost (i.e., the additional dollar cost, above the costs that would be incurred if the ships continued performing their currently assigned missions in the Indian Ocean/Persian Gulf region) might be small. However, there would be an opportunity cost in terms of those ships not performing their currently assigned missions in the Indian Ocean/Persian Gulf region. Such missions can include engagement activities aimed at building or reinforcing U.S. partnerships with other countries in the region, humanitarian assistance and disaster-response (HADR) operations, intelligence, surveillance, and reconnaissance (ISR) operations, counterterrorism operations, deterrence of regional aggression, and crisis response and containment. Policymakers might need to weigh the potential advantages of escorting U.S.- flagged commercial ships in the Gulf Aden against the potential disadvantages of reduced Navy capacity for performing other missions in the Indian Ocean/Persian Gulf region.

If Navy ships that are forward deployed to other regions, such as the Mediterranean or the Western Pacific, were diverted from their current missions in those regions to a mission of escorting U.S.-flagged commercial ships in the Gulf of Aden, the incremental financial cost could be larger due to the need to expend additional fuel to transit to and from the Gulf of Aden region. Even so, the incremental financial cost might be relatively small as a fraction of annual Navy costs for ship operations. There would again be an opportunity cost in terms of those ships not performing their currently assigned missions in the regions from which they were diverted, which again can include things such as engagement activities, HADR operations, ISR operations, counterterrorism operations, deterrence of regional aggression, and crisis response and containment. Policymakers might again need to weigh the potential advantages of escorting U.S.- flagged commercial ships in the Gulf Aden against the potential disadvantages of reduced Navy capacity for performing missions in areas such as the Mediterranean or Western Pacific.

Armed Security Details of U.S. Military Personnel

An alternative to having U.S. Navy (or Coast Guard) ships escort U.S.-flagged commercial ships would be to provide a small security detail of armed U.S. military personnel to each U.S.-flagged ship for the duration of its transit through the Gulf of Aden. The detail would board each U.S.- flagged ship at the start of its transit through the high-risk zone and depart the ship at the end of its transit through the high-risk zone. One person who has suggested this alternative—a retired U.S. Navy vice admiral—asserted that "A few well-armed teams aboard a few ships could accomplish this mission" of protecting U.S.-flagged commercial ships traveling through the area.[145] According to 2009 news reports, France placed military personnel aboard tuna fishing boats in the Indian Ocean and Belgium had offered eight-person military teams at a cost of $162,000 per week.[146] Some U.S. corporate officers have argued that military teams should protect U.S.-flagged in order to avoid "regulatory shortfalls, liability concerns, and international reluctance to permit armed merchant vessels into their ports."[147] Section 3506 of the House-passed version of H.R. 2647, the FY2010 Defense Authorization act, would have required the Secretary of Defense to embark U.S. military personnel on board U.S.-flagged vessels carrying cargos owned by the U.S. government if a vessel is traveling in a high risk area and is determined by the Coast Guard to be at risk of being boarded by pirates. The Senate version of the bill did not include these measures.

Maritime War Risk Insurance and Implications of "Armed Crews"

Standard hull and machinery insurance policies are not specifically designed to address security-related risks such as piracy. War Risk insurance provides this special coverage for ships exposed to piracy risks on a per transit basis. Federal law (Title XII of the Merchant Marine Act of 1936, as amended) authorizes the federal government to administer a maritime war risk insurance program that insures or reinsures, as a last resort, ocean-going commerce in high risk areas should private ocean marine insurance markets prove insufficient. Available statistics suggest that the insurance industry's financial resources are adequate, given policyholder surplus levels (an insurance term that refers to the claims-paying capacity or capital available to the insurer), and there is ample supply of coverage for ocean-going vessels.[148] As a result, despite the dramatic increase in piracy off the coast of Somalia and increased premiums for sending a cargo shipment through the Gulf of Aden, some may contend that Congress does not need to amend the existing federal insurance statutory construct.

As discussed above, some have urged the arming of ship crews or bringing onboard armed security as a risk mitigation option. Despite the persistence of pirate attacks, though, many ship owners and their underwriters are reluctant to employ armed security onboard their vessels. The use of armed security may create third-party liabilities if security officers harm innocent mariners or vessels. In March 2010, for the first time, private security guards aboard the *Almezaan* killed a Somali pirate attempting to attack a vessel. The *Almezaan* is a Panamanian-flagged cargo ship under United Arab Emirates-ownership.

Ocean marine insurers are divided on the "armed crew" issue. Some insurers believe that traditional negotiations after an act of piracy, which result in formula-based ransom payments and an understanding between ship owners and the pirates about not damaging the ship or cargo in exchange for expedited payments, are the best approach to containing the cost of ocean marine transportation in piracy zones. These insurers contend that arming ship crews would encourage pirates to be more violent when taking a ship, increasing the risks to cargo, vessels, and crew. Still others would support expanded self-defense efforts in an effort to protect international commerce, particularly as many struggle to recover from the recent global economic downturn.

Toward a Long-Term Solution: "Piracy is a Problem that Starts Ashore"[149]

Some Members of Congress have called on the Administration to develop a comprehensive approach to Somalia that responds to the threat of piracy in the context of a broader effort to stabilize the country and support transitional government institutions. Several U.S. officials have publicly supported such a holistic approach, arguing that a sustainable resolution to the threat of piracy off the Horn of Africa would require a combination of efforts to improve security, governance, the rule of law, and economic opportunity in Somalia.[150]

> "Ultimately, piracy is a problem that starts ashore and requires an international solution ashore. We made this clear at the offset of our efforts. We cannot guarantee safety in this vast region."
>
> Vice Admiral William Gortney
>
> Testimony of the Commander of U.S. Naval Forces Central Command before the House Armed Services Committee, March 5, 2009

The Obama Administration has repeatedly expressed its intention to continue working with partners in the Contact Group on Somalia and the Contact Group on Piracy off the Coast of Somalia toward those goals. In response to attacks on U.S.-flagged and -crewed vessels, a more robust anti-piracy policy has evolved, and official statements indicate that the Administration intends to proceed on a multi-track basis by building regional capacity, supporting multilateral anti-piracy initiatives, and improving coordination among U.S. government agencies involved.

The Administration's interagency Counter-Piracy Steering Group continues to lead the efforts of over 75 bureaus, offices, and embassies engaged in anti-piracy operations. The State and Defence Departments lead the Steering Group and the Departments of Transportation (U.S. Maritime Administration [MARAD]), Justice, Homeland Security, Treasury, and USAID are members. Enhanced U.S. assistance to the Somali governing institutions and engagement with regional Somali representatives also aims to strengthen the ability and willingness of Somalis to secure regions where pirates currently enjoy safe havens.

In the short term, the international community has primarily responded to the threat of piracy in the waters off the Horn of Africa with multinational naval patrols, diplomatic coordination, and enhanced self-protection and private security efforts by members of the commercial shipping industry. These efforts address two of the three lines of action identified in the U.S. government's action plan to address piracy, namely prevention and disruption of attacks. The third line of action, the prosecution of pirates, is considered by many to be a critical step toward addressing a perception of impunity among would-be offenders and making piracy less attractive. The challenge of locating and sustaining jurisdictions willing and able to prosecute piracy suspects and imprison those convicted, however, persists, despite some regional capacity building efforts.

In the long term, U.S. officials and international experts believe that addressing the threat of piracy will require the strengthening of regional security capabilities, improved intelligence gathering and sharing, more effective and capable law enforcement, and enhanced multilateral coordination, both at sea and on land. By all accounts, pirates will likely continue to find sanctuary in Somalia until basic governance and security conditions improve.

End Notes

[1] Statistical information on annual pirate attacks found in this report is derived from reports by the International Maritime Bureau, a division of the International Chamber of Commerce, unless otherwise indicated.

[2] The monsoon seasons in the Indian Ocean roughly correspond to December through February and June through August. Some studies suggest that weather patterns have not affected attack patterns in the Gulf of Aden. Bergen Risk Solutions, "Somali Piracy and the Monsoon Seasons," *World Piracy Update*, December 10, 2010.

[3] Of the 445 ships on which the IMB reported attempted or successful attacks globally by pirates in 2010, only four were U.S.-flagged, and, of those, only one, the *Maersk Alabama*, was attacked by Somali pirates. Somali pirates also attacked two U.S. naval vessels in 2010, the *U.S.S. Nicholas* and the *U.S.S. Ashland*.

[4] Warren Richey, "US Seizes Man in Somalia, Says He was Pirates' Negotiator in Fatal Hijacking," *The Christian Science Monitor*, April 13, 2011.

[5] For more information, see CRS Report R41455, *Piracy: A Legal Definition*, by R. Chuck Mason.

[6] "Somali Pirate Who Aided Attack on Ashland Gets 30 Years," *The Virginian-Pilot*, November 30, 2010.

[7] Guidance and advisories for U.S. vessels and can be found at http://homeport.uscg.mil/piracy and at http://www.marad.dot.gov/news_room_landing_page/horn_of_africa_piracy /horn_of_africa_piracy.htm.

[8] MARAD Advisory # 2011-01, Risk to Vessels Transiting High Risk Waters, February 25, 2011.

[9] The most recent version, *Best Management Practices 3*, can be found at http://www.marisec.org.

[10] Figures are projected totals of obligations for AMISOM support provided by U.S. State Department, February 2011.

[11] See, e.g., the International Crisis Group (ICG), *Somalia: The Transitional Government on Life Support*, Africa Report No. 170, February 21, 2011.

[12] U.N. Security Council (UNSC), *Report of the Secretary-General Pursuant to Security Council Resolution 1897 (2009)*, S/2010/556, October 27, 2010.

[13] UNSC, *Report of the Secretary-General on the Situation in Somalia*, S/2010/675, December 30, 2010.

[14] UNSC, *Report of the Special Advisor to the Secretary-General on Legal Issues Related to Piracy Off the Coast of Somalia*, S/2011/30, January 24, 2011.

[15] IMB data.

[16] *Report of the Secretary-General pursuant to Security Council Resolution 1846 (2008),* S/2009/146, March 16, 2009; International Expert Group on Piracy off the Somali Coast, *Final Report,* November 10-12, 2008, Nairobi, Kenya; *Report of the Monitoring Group on Somalia Pursuant to Security Council Resolution 1853 (2008)*, S/2010/91, March 10, 2010; S/2011/30, op. cit.

[17] S/2011/30, op. cit. Several of these instigators are identified in Executive Order 13536.

[18] In March 2010, S/2010/91 identified two primary pirate networks—one in central Somalia in the Mudug region districts of Harardhere and Hobyo, and another in the Puntland district of Garacad. The January 2011 S/2011/30 suggests that the original networks may have subsequently broken into smaller units.

[19] S/2011/30, op. cit.

[20] William Wechsler, Principal Deputy Assistant Secretary of State for Political and Military Affairs, Testimony before the House Transportation and Infrastructure Subcommittee on Coast Guard and Maritime Transportation, "The U.S. Response to Maritime Piracy," March 15. 2011.

[21] S/2010/91, op. cit.

[22] Report of the Secretary-General, S/2009/590, November 13, 2009. In April 2009, Puntland security forces began to launch raids on some alleged pirate bases, and the region's courts have tried and convicted suspected pirates. Local authorities also initiated *wa'yigelin,* a "sensitization campaign" and have offered general amnesty to those that renounce piracy. *All Africa*, "Anti-Piracy Campaign Begins Today in Puntland," April 24, 2009; and, *All Africa*, "Puntland Nabs 15 Pirate Suspects, Seizes 5 Boats," May 18, 2009.

[23] For more information, see ICG, *Somalia: The Transitional Government on Life Support*, op. cit.

[24] The dire economic and security situation in Somalia is illustrated by the continuing outflow of refugees and migrants to neighboring countries. The U.N. High Commissioner for Refugees estimates that there are as many as 170,000 registered refugees, mostly Somali, in Yemen, and unofficial figures are estimated to be much higher. Hundreds of migrants die in boat accidents each year in the Gulf of Aden while trying to cross to Yemen

[25] International Expert Group on Piracy off the Somali Coast, *Final Report*, op. cit.

[26] General Insurance Research Organizing (Committee; GIRO) estimate, as referenced in Anna Bowden et al., *The Economic Cost of Maritime Piracy*, One Earth Future Working Paper, December 2010.

[27] The U.N. experts group noted the tendency of pirates to characterize their actions as an alternative livelihood or as retribution for illegal international activities in Somali waters: "The pirates also firmly believe that they have every right and entitlement to attack illegal fishing vessels operating in their territorial waters as their fishing resources are being pillaged daily by international shipping vessels from Asia and Europe." International Expert Group on Piracy off the Somali Coast, *Final Report*, p. 15.

[28] S/2011/30, op. cit. See also a July 2005 report from the United Kingdom Department for International Development (DFID), "Review of Impacts of Illegal, Unreported and Unregulated Fishing on Developing Countries," which estimated that Somalis lost $100 million to illegal tuna and shrimp fishing in the country's exclusive economic zone in 2003-2004.

[29] *Statement of the Contact Group on Piracy off the Coast of Somalia*, New York, January 14, 2009.

[30] "Somali Piracy 'Reduces Tuna Haul,'" BBC, January 22, 2009; "Yemen Losses Reach US$ 150 Mln Due to Piracy in 2009," Saba Net, October 27, 2010.

[31] The U.S. government has provided mariners with descriptions of common pirate tactics and instructions for response. See, for example, U.S. Department of Transportation Maritime Administration, "Somali Pirate Tactics," December 2008 available at http://www.marad.dot.gov/documents/HOA_Somali%20Pirate%20Tactics_15DEC2008.pdf.

[32] Assistant Secretary Andrew J. Shapiro, U.S. State Department, Bureau of Political-Military Affairs, "Taking Diplomatic Action Against Piracy," Remarks to the Global Maritime Information Sharing Symposium, National Defense University, Washington, D.C., September 16, 2009.

[33] For a detailed account of this share-based distribution system among pirates, see Annex III of the Report of the Monitoring Group on Somalia pursuant to Security Council Resolution 1853 (2008), S/2010/91, March 10, 2010.

[34] International Chamber of Commerce- International Maritime Bureau, "Shipping Industry dismisses reports of targeted Somali pirate attacks," May 15, 2009.

[35] U.S. Office of Naval Intelligence, Maritime OPINTEL Report—SOMALIA: Piracy Analysis and Warning Weekly (PAWW) Report (Horn of Africa), March 17, 2010.

[36] Comments by Admiral Mark Fitzgerald in "Work with Yemen Government on Somali Piracy: U.S. Admiral," *Reuters*, March 9, 2009.

[37] Anna Bowden et al., *The Economic Cost of Maritime Piracy*, One Earth Future Working Paper, December 2010.

[38] According to IMB data, 13 of the over 1,000 hostages taken by Somali pirates in 2010 were injured (8 were killed). Pirates in other parts of the world who engage in these types of attacks may be more likely to kill or seriously wound merchant ship crew members, since extracting ransom payments is not their primary objective.

[39] "Report: Somali Pirates Torturing Hostages," Associated Press, February 2, 2011.

[40] U.S. Office of Naval Intelligence, Maritime OPINTEL Report—SOMALIA: Piracy Analysis and Warning Weekly (PAWW) Report (Horn of Africa), December 16, 2010.

[41] The April 14, 2009, attack on the U.S.-flagged *Liberty Sun* allegedly was carried out with the intention of damaging or sinking the ship and injuring or killing its crew in retaliation for the deaths of three Somali pirates during U.S. military efforts to secure the release of the detained captain of the *Maersk Alabama* days earlier. Agence France Presse, "Pirates stage rocket attack on US freighter," April 14, 2009.

[42] Others onboard were rescued safely. The French military also has reportedly undertaken a number of raid and rescue operations to free its citizens held aboard seized ships.

[43] According to the African Development Bank, Puntland government revenues were $16 million in 2009, Somaliland revenues were $22 million.

[44] U.S. Department of Energy, Energy Information Administration, *Country Analysis Brief: World Oil Transit Chokepoints*, February 2011.

[45] U.S. Department of Transportation, Maritime Administration, Statement of Acting Deputy Administrator James Caponti before the House Committee on Transportation and Infrastructure Subcommittee on Coast Guard and Maritime Transportation, February 4, 2009.

[46] Anna Bowden et al., *The Economic Cost of Maritime Piracy*, One Earth Future Working Paper, December 2010.

[47] For more information about the commercial impact of piracy, see CRS Report R40081, *Ocean Piracy and Its Impact on Insurance*, by Rawle O. King.

[48] See Financial Express, "Piracy Pushes Up Insurance Premiums for Ship Owners," March 14, 2011, located at: [http://www.hellenicshippingnews.com/index.php?option=com_content&view=article&id=12634:piracy-pushes-upinsurance-premiums-for-ship-owners&catid=44:latest-news&Itemid=64].

[49] Ibid.

[50] Hull and machinery insurance is a type of marine insurance that covers physical loss or damage to a vessel.

[51] Robert F. Worth, "Pirates Seize Saudi Tanker off Kenya: Ship Called the Largest Ever Hijacked," *New York Times*, November 18, 2008.

[52] Stuart Collins, "Insurers Increase War Rates for Several High-Risk Areas," *Business Insurance*, September 7, 2009.

[53] Zack Phillips, "Marine Insurers Transfer Piracy Risk to War Cover: Surge in Attacks Prompts Move by London market," *Business Insurance,* March 30, 2009.

[54] U.S. Assistant Secretary of State for Political-Military Affairs Andrew J. Shapiro, Keynote Address to American University Law Review Symposium—Counter-Piracy Policy: Delivering Judicial Consequences, Washington, DC, March 31, 2010.

[55] Food insecurity is also exacerbated by banditry, roadblocks, inter-clan fighting, and attacks on aid workers.

[56] USAID, *Complex Emergency—Ethiopia, Fact Sheet #1*, January 12, 2011.

[57] The *U.S.S. Bainbridge* is named for Captain William Bainbridge, the commander of the *U.S.S. Philadelphia* who was held in captivity in the Barbary state of Tripoli from 1803 to 1805 after the *Philadelphia* ran aground in Tripoli harbor during anti-piracy operations. The captivity of Bainbridge and his crew significantly escalated the military confrontation between the United States and the Barbary pirates, whose threats to U.S. vessels in the Mediterranean were a key factor in the early development of the United States Navy. For more information, see http://www.bainbridge.navy.mil/sitepages/history.aspx.

[58] See complaint U.S. v. Abduwali Abdukhadir Muse, 09-MG-1012, U.S. District Court, Southern District of New York, April 21, 2009; and Alexandra Marks, "Teen Somali to be Tried as Adult," *Christian Science Monitor*, April 21, 2009. Muse was charged with participating in two other pirate attacks in January 2010. He pled not guilty.

[59] Agence France Presse, "Pirates stage rocket attack on US freighter," April 14, 2009.

[60] ICG, *Somalia: The Trouble with Puntland,* Africa Briefing No. 64, August 12, 2009; Sally Healy and Ginny Hill, *Yemen and Somalia: Terrorism, Shadow Networks and the Limitations of State-Building*, Chatham House, October 2010.

[61] Vice Admiral William Gortney, Commander, U.S. Naval Forces Central Command, told the House Armed Services Committee on March 5, 2009, that "We look very, very carefully for a linkage between piracy and terrorism or any kind of ideology and we do not see it. It would be a significant game changer should that linkage occur. But we have not seen it. We watch very carefully for it."

[62] Stewart Bell, "Somali militants training pirates," *National Post* (Toronto), December 03, 2009.

[63] S/2011/30, op. cit.

[64] "Somali Rebels Detail Several Pirate Gang Leaders," Reuters, February 17, 2011; and "Somali Rebels Agree Ransom Deal with Pirate Leaders," Reuters, February 22, 2011.

[65] William Wechsler, Principal Deputy Assistant Secretary of State for Political and Military Affairs, Testimony before the House Transportation and Infrastructure Subcommittee on Coast Guard and Maritime Transportation, "The U.S. Response to Maritime Piracy," March 15. 2011.

[66] Jeffrey Gettleman, "Guards for Somali Leader Join Islamists," *New York Times*, July 22, 2010; and Gettleman, "In Somalia, a Leader Is Raising Hopes for Stability," *New York Times*, September 17, 2009.

[67] UNSC, "Countering Piracy off the Horn of Africa: Partnership and Action Plan," December 2008, available at http://www.marad.dot.gov/documents/Countering_Piracy_Off_The_Horn_of_Africa_-_Partnership__Action_Plan.pdf.

[68] U.S. State Department, "The United States Signs "New York Declaration," Washington, DC, September 9, 2009.

[69] Donna Hopkins, Plans and Policy Team Leader, U.S. State Department Bureau of Political-Military Affairs, Office of Plans, Policy, and Analysis, "Safeguarding the Seaways: Counter-Piracy Contact Group Meets in New York," *Dipnote*, September 17, 2009.

[70] Secretary of State Hillary Clinton, "Announcement of Counter-Piracy Initiatives," Washington, DC, April 15, 2009.

[71] State Department Bureau of Political Military Affairs, Maritime Security Sector Reform Guide, December 2010.

[72] GAO, "Maritime Security: Actions Needed to Assess and Update Plan and Enhance Collaboration among Partners Involved in Countering Piracy off the Horn of Africa," GAO-10-856, September 24, 2010.

[73] For more information, see the Committee web page at http://www.un.org/sc/committees/751/.

[74] See S/2010/394, July 26, 2010. "Option 1: The enhancement of United Nations assistance to build capacity of regional States to prosecute and imprison persons responsible for acts of piracy and armed robbery at sea off the coast of Somalia; Option 2: The establishment of a Somali court sitting in the territory of a third State in the region, either with or without United Nations participation; Option 3: The establishment of a special chamber within the national jurisdiction of a State or States in the region, without United Nations participation; Option 4: The establishment of a special chamber within the national jurisdiction of a State or States in the region, with United Nations participation; Option 5: The establishment of a

regional tribunal on the basis of a multilateral agreement among regional States, with United Nations participation; Option 6: The establishment of an international tribunal on the basis of an agreement between a State in the region and the United Nations; Option 7: The establishment of an international tribunal by Security Council resolution under Chapter VII of the Charter of the United Nations."

[75] Convention on the High Seas, 13 U.S.T. 2312; T.I.A.S. 5200; 450 U.N.T.S. 82. Signed at Geneva, April 29, 1958. Entered into force September 30, 1962; United Nations Convention on the Law of the Seas (UNCLOS), 21 I.L.M. 1261. Convention adopted December 10, 1982. Entered into force November 16, 1994 (the United States is not a party to the Agreement); and Convention for the Suppression of Unlawful Acts Against the Safety of Maritime Navigation, T.I.A.S. Signed at Rome, March 10, 1988. Entered into force March 1, 1992 (for the United States March 6, 1995).

[76] The United Nations Convention on the Law of the Sea (A historical perspective), available at http://www.un.org/Depts/los/convention_agreements/convention_historical_perspective.htm.

[77] Convention on the High Seas at Article 14; UNCLOS at Article 100.

[78] UNCLOS at Article 101. (The definition is, with a minor grammatical change, the same definition found in the Convention on the High Seas (Article 14).

[79] Convention on the High Seas at Article 22.

[80] Convention on the High Seas at Article 19; UNCLOS at Article 105.

[81] *Id.*

[82] International Maritime Organization statement on aims for the Convention for the Suppression of Unlawful Acts Against the Safety of Maritime Navigation, available at http://www.imo.org/.

[83] *Id.*

[84] Convention for the Suppression of Unlawful Acts Against the Safety of Maritime Navigation at Article 5.

[85] 18 U.S.C. § 1651 *et seq.*

[86] 18 U.S.C. §§ 1651 and 1652.

[87] Resolution 1851 "encourages all States and regional organizations fighting piracy and armed robbery at sea off the coast of Somalia to establish an international cooperation mechanism to act as a common point of contact... on all aspects of combating piracy and armed robbery at sea off Somalia's coast."

[88] *Statement of the Contact Group on Piracy off the Coast of Somalia*, New York, January 14, 2009.

[89] Communiqué, of the Seventh Plenary Meeting of the Contact Group on Piracy off the Coast of Somalia, November 17, 2010. Available at: http://www.state.gov/t/pm/rls/othr/misc/151795.htm.

[90] The International Maritime Organization is a United Nations agency with over 168 member governments. Based in the United Kingdom, its members develop regulations for international shipping related to safety, the environment, and maritime security. It also serves as a global coordinating body for legal issues, technical co-operation, and maritime security including anti-piracy efforts. For more information, see: http://www.imo.org/.

[91] IMO Resolution A.1002(25) "calls Upon Governments in the region to conclude, in co-operation with the Organization, and implement, as soon as possible, a regional agreement to prevent, deter and suppress piracy and armed robbery against ships."

[92] Resolution 1851 "encourages all states and regional organizations fighting piracy and armed robbery at sea off the coast of Somalia to consider creating a center in the region to

coordinate information relevant to piracy and armed robbery at sea off the coast of Somalia."

[93] Meeting minutes available at http://www.fco.gov.uk/resources/en/pdf/pdf9/piracy-djibouti-meeting.

[94] Djibouti, Ethiopia, Kenya, Madagascar, Maldives, Seychelles, Somalia, the United Republic of Tanzania, and Yemen signed the code of conduct in January 2009. Sixteen states had signed the document as of October 2010.

[95] Text available at http://www.recaap.org/about/pdf/ReCAAP%20Agreement.pdf.

[96] A diagram of ReCAAP-ISC reporting and response procedures is available at http://www.recaap.org/about/pdf/ Information_Flow_Response_chart.pdf.

[97] One knot is unit of measurement equivalent to one nautical mile per hour or 1.15 miles per hour.

[98] The term 'freeboard' refers to the distance between the waterline and the main deck of the ship.

[99] U.S. Office of Naval Intelligence, Maritime OPINTEL Report—SOMALIA: Piracy Analysis and Warning Weekly (PAWW) Report (Horn of Africa), March 17, 2010.

[100] Best Management Practices to Deter Piracy in the Gulf of Aden and off the Coast of Somalia, Version 2, August 2009, available at http://www.icc-ccs.org/images/stories/pdfs/bmp 21-8-2009.pdf.

[101] Available at http://www.icc-ccs.org/index.php?option=com_content&view=article&id=344&Itemid=233.

[102] U.S. Department of Transportation, Maritime Administration Advisory # 2010-06, Guidance to Vessels Transiting High Risk Waters, March 29, 2010.

[103] Greg Torode, "Pirates Seize Chinese Crew in Arabian Sea," *South China Morning Post*, November 14, 2010.

[104] NATO Allied Maritime Component Command, "NATO works with Somali officials," August 14, 2009, available at http://www.manw.nato.int/page_operation_ocean_shield.aspx.

[105] European Union Council Secretariat, "Fact Sheet: EU naval operation against piracy (EU NAVFOR Somalia— Operation ATALANTA)," EU NAVFOR/04, March 2009.

[106] Information on the Maritime Security Center-Horn of Africa (MSC-HOA) is available at http://www.mschoa.eu/Default.aspx.

[107] UNSC, *Report of the Special Adviser to the Secretary-General on Legal Issues Related to Piracy off the Coast of Somalia,* S/2011/30, January 25, 2011.

[108] "Pirates Jailed in 17 Nations As Prosecutions Rise," Associated Press, March 15, 2011.

[109] Agence France Presse, "To fight pirate scourge, follow the money: US admiral," April 16, 2010.

[110] S/2010/675, op. cit.

[111] Resolution 1851 "invites" states and regional organizations "to conclude special agreements or arrangements with countries willing to take custody of pirates in order to embark law enforcement officials ("shipriders") from the latter countries, in particular countries in the region, to facilitate the investigation and prosecution of persons detained as a result of operations conducted under [the] resolution."

[112] Secretary of State Hillary Clinton, Hearing on the Proposed FY2012 Budget Request for the State Department by the Senate Appropriations Subcommittee on State Foreign Operations and Related Programs, March 2, 2011.

[113] Ibid.

[114] Testimony of Ray Mabus, Secretary, Department of the Navy, "Proposed Fiscal 2012 Budget for the U.S. Navy," Hearing by the Senate Armed Services Committee, March 8, 2011.

[115] The report was delivered on February 26, 2010. It details a number of steps the Administration has taken to issue guidelines to U.S.-flagged vessels and to coordinate with regional port authorities to determine regulatory requirements relevant to armed security personnel.

[116] GAO, "Maritime Security: Actions Needed to Assess and Update Plan and Enhance Collaboration among Partners Involved in Countering Piracy off the Horn of Africa," GAO-10-856, September 24, 2010.

[117] AFRICOM's AOR includes all African countries except Egypt, which remained in CENTCOM's AOR after responsibilities for DOD activities in the Horn of Africa were transferred to AFRICOM in 2008. See CRS Report
CRS Report RL34003, *Africa Command: U.S. Strategic Interests and the Role of the U.S. Military in Africa*, by Lauren Ploch.

[118] U.S. AFRICOM/Republic of Seychelles, Office of the President, "Seychelles President James Michel Hails Strengthening of Surveillance Cooperation with the United States," August 20, 2009.

[119] Testimony of then-Acting Undersecretary of State for International Security and Arms Control Stephen Mull before the House Armed Services Committee, March 5, 2009.

[120] Unclassified U.S. Department of State diplomatic correspondence, January 2001. The contract ended in 2001 when Puntland's civil war resulted in the maritime security force splitting along factional lines.

[121] Theodore Richard, "Reconsidering the Letter of Marque: Utilizing Private Security Providers Against Piracy," *Public Contract Law Journal*, Vol. 39, No. 3., Spring 2010.

[122] Stig Jarle Hansen, "Private Security and Local Politics in Somalia," *Review of African Political Economy*, Vol. 35 Issue 118, December 2008.

[123] "US Firm to Fight Somali Pirates," BBC, November 25, 2005; and Chris Tomlinson, "US: DynCorp Hired for Somalia Peacekeeping," *Forbes*, March 7, 2007. The TFG engaged other firms to secure the coastline but the contracts were never implemented, according to Richard, "Reconsidering the Letter of Marque: Utilizing Private Security Providers Against Piracy," op. cit.

[124] Statement issued by the Communications Office of the Puntland Presidency as reported on the Alashid Network, online at http://english.alshahid.net/archives/15361.

[125] See, e.g., "Secret Donor Pays for Somali Militia," *Los Angeles Times*, December 2, 2010.

[126] For one review and discussion of these legal questions from a U.S. military point of view, see Cmdr. James Kraska and Capt. Brian Wilson, "Fighting Piracy," *Armed Forces Journal*, February 1, 2009 (expressing view that international and regional cooperation, not armed force, is the long-term solution to piracy).

[127] *See* http://www.smh.com.au/world/fate-of-teen-pirate-uncertain-20090414-a5ih.html.

[128] For example, under common law, children under the age of seven are conclusively presumed to be without criminal capacity, those who have reached the age of fourteen are treated as fully responsible, while as to those between the ages of seven and fourteen there is a rebuttable presumption of criminal incapacity. In addition jurisdictions have adopted juvenile court legislation providing that some or all criminal conduct by those persons under a certain age (usually eighteen) must or may be adjudicated in the juvenile court rather than in a criminal proceeding. LaFave & Scott, Criminal Law §4.11 (2d ed. 1986).

[129] Kenya adopted a new Merchant Shipping Act in 2009. Some reports suggest that legal deficiencies in the Act resulted in the November 2010 High Court ruling, in which 9 suspected pirates were released.

[130] U.S. Department of Transportation Maritime Administration Advisories are available at http://www.marad.dot.gov/news_room_landing_page/maritime_advisories/advisory_summary.htm.

[131] Most of the concerns listed here are discussed in John W. Miller and Paulo Prada, "Attack Raises Debate On Guns For Sailors," *Wall Street Journal*, April 11, 2009; and Keith Bradsher, "Rescue Fuels Debate Over Arming Crews," *New York Times*, April 13, 2009.

[132] Katharine Houreld, "Private Ship Escorts Guard Against Pirates," *NavyTimes.com*, June 5, 2009. For additional discussions of issues relating to arming of merchant ships, see Keith Bradsher, "Rescue Fuels Debate Over Arming Crews," *New York Times*, April 13, 2009; and John W. Miller and Paulo Prada, "Attack Raises Debate On Guns For Sailors," *Wall Street Journal*, April 11, 2009.

[133] Revised guidance on combating piracy agreed by IMO Maritime Safety Committee, Maritime Safety Committee— 86th session: 27 May - 5 June 2009.

[134] Report to Congress on Restrictions on U.S.-Flagged Commercial Vessel Security Pursuant to P.L. 111-84, Section 3506, February 26, 2010. Report provided to CRS by U.S. Navy Office of Legislative Affairs, April 2010.

[135] P.L. 90-629, 90 Stat. 744 (22 U.S.C. § 2778) (Arms export control is addressed in Chapter 39 of Title 22 of the *United States Code* (22 U.S.C. §§ 2751-2799aa-2)).

[136] 22 C.F.R. §§ 120-130.

[137] A 'U.S. person' is defined at 22 C.F.R. §120.14 and §120.15, as a "natural person who is a lawful permanent resident as defined by 8 U.S.C. § 1101(a)(20) or who is a protected person as defined by 8 U.S.C. § 1324b(a)(3). It also means any corporation, business association, partnership, society, trust, or any other entity, organization or group that is incorporated to do business in the United States. It also includes any governmental (federal, state, local) entity."

[138] 22 C.F.R. pt. 121.

[139] The term 'United States' is defined at 22 C.F.R. § 120.13, as "when used in the geographical sense, includes the several states, the Commonwealth of Puerto Rico, the insular possession of the United States, the District of Columbia, the Commonwealth of the North Mariana Islands, any territory or possession over which the United States exercises any powers of administration, legislation, and jurisdiction."

[140] 22 C.F.R. § 120.17(a).

[141] 22 C.F.R. § 121.1.

[142] 22 C.F.R. § 123.18(c).

[143] *Id.*

[144] 22 C.F.R. § 126.1.

[145] John B. Perkins III, "Protect Our Mariners," *Washington Times*, August 30, 2009: B1.

[146] Christopher Torchia, "Western Nations Weigh Arming Civilian Ships," *NavyTimes.com*, August 13, 2009.

[147] Testimony of Arthur J. Volkle, Jr., Vice President, American Cargo Transport, Inc., before the House Committee on Transportation and Infrastructure Subcommittee on Coast Guard and Maritime Transportation, May 20, 2009.

[148] According to the A.M. Best Company, the U.S. property/casualty insurance industry's reported surplus, a measure of claims-paying capacity or capital, increased by $45.5 billion to $556.9 billion in 2010, up from $511.4 billion in 2009. While not all of the $556.9 billion is allocated to ocean marine insurance, the level of industry-wide surplus suggests U.S. private insurers have the overall financial resources to cover potential losses from incidences of ocean piracy.

[149] United States Navy, Commander, Combined Maritime Forces Public Affairs, "Combined Maritime Forces Issues New Alert to Mariners," April 7, 2009.

[150] Dr. Jun Bando, Maritime Security Coordinator/U.S. Africa Command Liaison, U.S. Department of State Bureau of African Affairs, "International Response to Piracy Expanded, Unified," *DipNote*, January 30, 2009.

INDEX

D

E

H

I

J

K

L

M

N

O

P

Q

R

S

T